FREE FROM SHAME

HOW THE GOSPEL REDEEMS OUR PAST AND PAIN

THIS STUDY BELONGS TO:

_____

_____

THE DAILY GRACE CO.®

Free From Shame: How the Gospel Redeems Our Past and Pain
Copyright © 2024 by The Daily Grace Co.®
Spring, Texas. All rights reserved.

Unless otherwise noted, all Scripture quotations are taken from the Christian Standard Bible®, Copyright © 2020 by Holman Bible Publishers. Used by permission. Christian Standard Bible® and CSB® are federally registered trademarks of Holman Bible Publishers.

The Daily Grace Co.® exists to equip disciples to know and love God and His Word by creating beautiful, theologically rich, and accessible resources so that God may be glorified and the gospel made known.

Designed in the United States of America and printed in China.

God will *come after* the ashamed. He does not leave us to suffer *alone* under the dark cloud.

TABLE OF CONTENTS

◆ Introduction

Study Suggestions	6	*Timeline of Scripture*	12
How to Study the Bible	8	*Metanarrative of Scripture*	14
The Attributes of God	10		

◆ Week One

Scripture Memory	18	*End-of-Week Reflection*	52
Day One	20	*Week One Application*	54

◆ Week Two

Scripture Memory	58	*End-of-Week Reflection*	90
Day One	60	*Week Two Application*	94

◆ Week Three

Scripture Memory	98	*End-of-Week Reflection*	130
Day One	100	*Week Three Application*	134

◆ Week Four

Scripture Memory	138	*End-of-Week Reflection*	174
Day One	140	*Week Four Application*	176

◆ Extras

Scriptures for Facing Forgiveness	44	*Identifying and Replacing Thoughts of Shame*	152
Image-Bearers Once More	92		
Shame in Jesus's Family	132	*What is the Gospel?*	180

STUDY READING PLAN

Week One — Scripture Memory: 2 Corinthians 5:17

DAY 1	INTRODUCTION – WHAT IS SHAME?
DAY 2	SHAME AND THE CURSE
DAY 3	SHAME AND THE PAST
DAY 4	SHAME AND RELATIONSHIPS
DAY 5	SHAME AND IDENTITY + END-OF-WEEK REFLECTION
DAYS 6 + 7	WEEK ONE APPLICATION

Week Two — Scripture Memory: John 4:13–14

DAY 1	HAGAR: REJECTED TO RECEIVED
DAY 2	HANNAH: DISTRESSED TO REJOICING
DAY 3	GOMER: UNFAITHFUL TO RESTORED
DAY 4	WOMAN WITH THE ISSUE OF BLOOD: SICK TO HEALED
DAY 5	WOMAN AT THE WELL: CONDEMNED TO REDEEMED + END-OF-WEEK REFLECTION
DAYS 6 + 7	WEEK TWO APPLICATION

Week Three — Scripture Memory: Philippians 3:8

DAY 1	ZACCHAEUS: OUTCAST TO ACCEPTED
DAY 2	A MAN BORN BLIND: BLAMED TO FREED
DAY 3	PETER: WAYWARD TO COMMISSIONED
DAY 4	PAUL: SELF-RIGHTEOUS TO HUMBLE
DAY 5	JESUS: BORE OUR SHAME + END-OF-WEEK REFLECTION
DAYS 6 + 7	WEEK THREE APPLICATION

Week Four — Scripture Memory: Romans 8:1–2

DAY 1	GOD'S PROMISES IN CHRIST FOR THE ASHAMED
DAY 2	FIGHTING THOUGHTS OF SHAME
DAY 3	RESTING IN THE WORK OF CHRIST
DAY 4	RECEIVING THE GRACE OF GOD
DAY 5	HOPE FOR SHAME + END-OF-WEEK REFLECTION
DAYS 6 + 7	WEEK FOUR APPLICATION

STUDY SUGGESTIONS

We believe that the Bible is true, trustworthy, and timeless and that it is vitally important for all believers. These study suggestions are intended to help you more effectively study Scripture as you seek to know and love God through His Word.

SUGGESTED STUDY TOOLS

Bible

Double-spaced, printed copy of the Scripture passages that this study covers (You can use a website like www.biblegateway.com to copy the text of a passage and print out a double-spaced copy to be able to mark on easily.)

Journal to write notes or prayers

Pens, colored pencils, and highlighters

Dictionary to look up unfamiliar words

HOW TO USE THIS STUDY

Pray

Begin your study time in prayer. Ask God to reveal Himself to you, help you understand what you are reading, and transform you with His Word (Psalm 119:18).

Read Scripture

Before you read what is written in each day of the study itself, read the assigned passages of Scripture for that day. Use your double-spaced copy to circle, underline, highlight, draw arrows, and mark in any way you would like to help you dig deeper as you work through a passage.

Memorize Scripture

Each week of the study begins with a memory verse. You may want to write the verse down and place it somewhere you will see it often. We also recommend spending a few minutes memorizing the verse before you complete each day's study material.

Read Study Content

Read the daily written content provided for the current study day.

Respond

Answer the questions that appear at the end of each study day.

HOW TO STUDY THE BIBLE

The inductive method provides tools for deeper and more intentional Bible study. To study the Bible inductively, work through the steps below after reading background information on the book.

Observation + Comprehension
KEY QUESTION: WHAT DOES THE TEXT SAY?

After reading the daily Scripture in its entirety at least once, begin working with smaller portions of the Scripture. Read a passage of Scripture repetitively, and then mark the following items in the text:

- *Key or repeated words and ideas*
- *Key themes*
- *Transition words (e.g., therefore, but, because, if/then, likewise, etc.)*
- *Lists*
- *Comparisons and contrasts*
- *Commands*
- *Unfamiliar words (look these up in a dictionary)*
- *Questions you have about the text*

Interpretation
KEY QUESTION: WHAT DOES THE TEXT MEAN?

Once you have annotated the text, work through the following steps to help you interpret its meaning:

- *Read the passage in other versions for a better understanding of the text.*
- *Read cross-references to help interpret Scripture with Scripture.*
- *Paraphrase or summarize the passage to check for understanding.*
- *Identify how the text reflects the metanarrative of Scripture, which is the story of creation, fall, redemption, and restoration.*
- *Read trustworthy commentaries if you need further insight into the meaning of the passage.*

Application

KEY QUESTION: HOW SHOULD THE TRUTH OF THIS PASSAGE CHANGE ME?

Bible study is not merely an intellectual pursuit. The truths about God, ourselves, and the gospel that we discover in Scripture should produce transformation in our hearts and lives. Answer the following questions and prompts as you consider what you have learned in your study:

- *What attributes of God's character are revealed in the passage?*
- *Consider places where the text directly states the character of God, as well as how His character is revealed through His words and actions.*
- *What do I learn about myself in light of who God is?*
- *Consider how you fall short of God's character, how the text reveals your sin nature, and what it says about your new identity in Christ.*
- *How should this truth change me?*
- *A passage of Scripture may contain direct commands telling us what to do or warnings about sins to avoid in order to help us grow in holiness. Other times, our application flows out of seeing ourselves in light of God's character. As we pray and reflect on how God is calling us to change in light of His Word, we should be asking questions like, "How should I pray for God to change my heart?" and "What practical steps can I take toward cultivating habits of holiness?"*

THE ATTRIBUTES OF GOD

Eternal

God has no beginning and no end. He always was, always is, and always will be.

HAB. 1:12 / REV. 1:8 / IS. 41:4

Faithful

God is incapable of anything but fidelity. He is loyally devoted to His plan and purpose.

2 TIM. 2:13 / DEUT. 7:9 / HEB. 10:23

Good

God is pure; there is no defilement in Him. He is unable to sin, and all He does is good.

GEN. 1:31 / PS. 34:8 / PS. 107:1

Gracious

God is kind, giving us gifts and benefits we do not deserve.

**2 KINGS 13:23 / PS. 145:8
IS. 30:18**

Holy

God is undefiled and unable to be in the presence of defilement. He is sacred and set-apart.

REV. 4:8 / LEV. 19:2 / HAB. 1:13

Incomprehensible and Transcendent

God is high above and beyond human understanding. He is unable to be fully known.

**PS. 145:3 / IS. 55:8-9
ROM. 11:33-36**

Immutable

God does not change. He is the same yesterday, today, and tomorrow.

**1 SAM. 15:29 / ROM. 11:29
JAMES 1:17**

Infinite

God is limitless. He exhibits all of His attributes perfectly and boundlessly.

**ROM. 11:33-36 / IS. 40:28
PS. 147:5**

Jealous

God is desirous of receiving the praise and affection He rightly deserves.

**EX. 20:5 / DEUT. 4:23-24
JOSH. 24:19**

Just

God governs in perfect justice. He acts in accordance with justice. In Him, there is no wrongdoing or dishonesty.

IS. 61:8 / DEUT. 32:4 / PS. 146:7-9

Loving

God is eternally, enduringly, steadfastly loving and affectionate. He does not forsake or betray His covenant love.

JN. 3:16 / EPH. 2:4-5 / 1 JN. 4:16

Merciful

God is compassionate, withholding from us the wrath that we deserve.

**TITUS 3:5 / PS. 25:10
LAM. 3:22-23**

Omnipotent
God is all-powerful; His strength is unlimited.
MAT. 19:26 / JOB 42:1-2
JER. 32:27

Omnipresent
God is everywhere; His presence is near and permeating.
PROV. 15:3 / PS. 139:7-10
JER. 23:23-24

Omniscient
God is all-knowing; there is nothing unknown to Him.
PS. 147:4 / I JN. 3:20
HEB. 4:13

Patient
God is long-suffering and enduring. He gives ample opportunity for people to turn toward Him.
ROM. 2:4 / 2 PET. 3:9 / PS. 86:15

Self-Existent
God was not created but exists by His power alone.
PS. 90:1-2 / JN. 1:4 / JN. 5:26

Self-Sufficient
God has no needs and depends on nothing, but everything depends on God.
IS. 40:28-31 / ACTS 17:24-25
PHIL. 4:19

Sovereign
God governs over all things; He is in complete control.
COL. 1:17 / PS. 24:1-2
1 CHRON. 29:11-12

Truthful
God is our measurement of what is fact. By Him we are able to discern true and false.
JN. 3:33 / ROM. 1:25 / JN. 14:6

Wise
God is infinitely knowledgeable and is judicious with His knowledge.
IS. 46:9-10 / IS. 55:9 / PROV. 3:19

Wrathful
God stands in opposition to all that is evil. He enacts judgment according to His holiness, righteousness, and justice.
PS. 69:24 / JN. 3:36 / ROM. 1:18

The Attributes of God — 11

TIMELINE OF SCRIPTURE

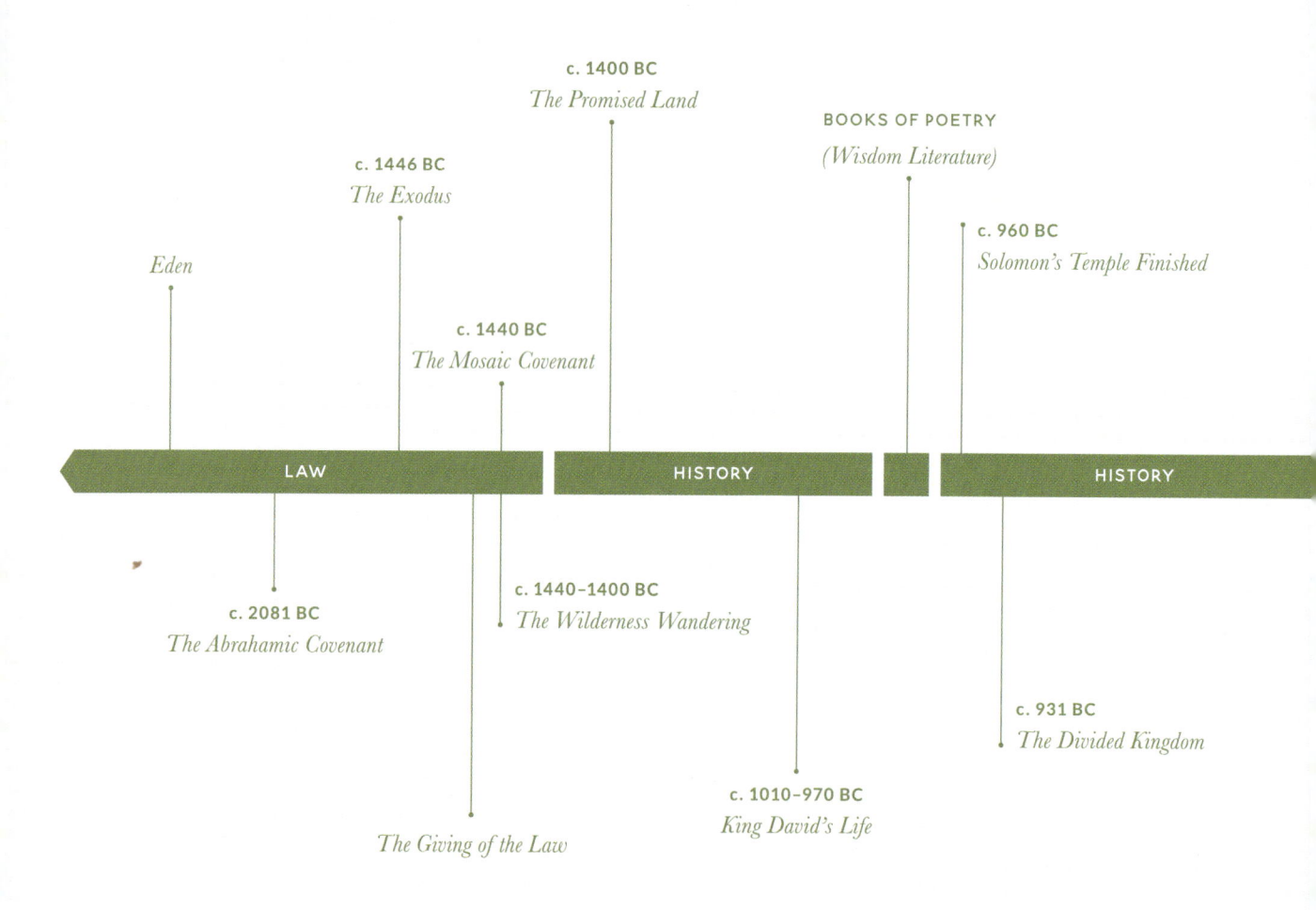

Eden

c. 2081 BC
The Abrahamic Covenant

LAW

c. 1446 BC
The Exodus

c. 1440 BC
The Mosaic Covenant

The Giving of the Law

c. 1440–1400 BC
The Wilderness Wandering

c. 1400 BC
The Promised Land

HISTORY

c. 1010–970 BC
King David's Life

BOOKS OF POETRY
(Wisdom Literature)

c. 960 BC
Solomon's Temple Finished

HISTORY

c. 931 BC
The Divided Kingdom

Timeline of Scripture

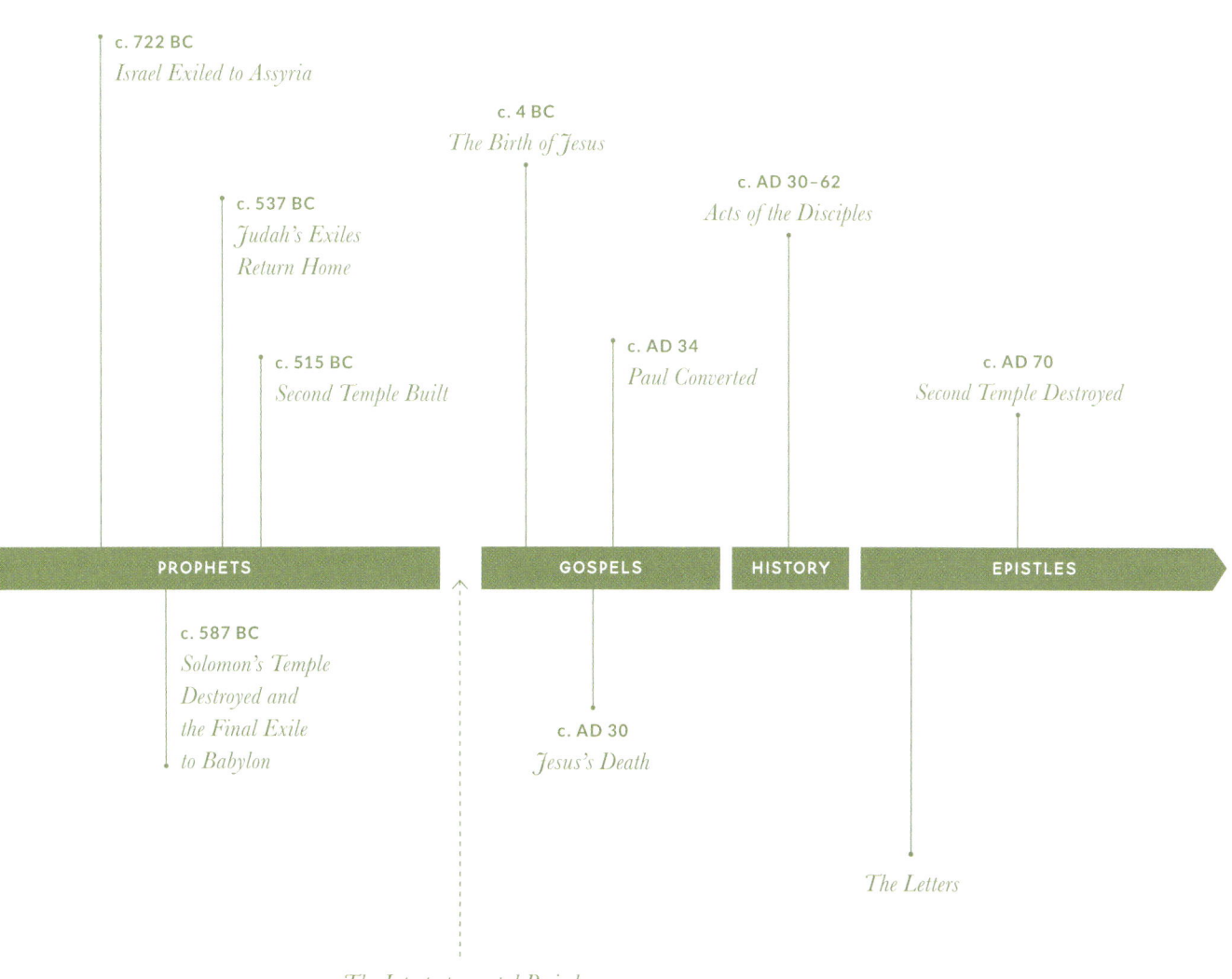

c. 722 BC
Israel Exiled to Assyria

c. 537 BC
Judah's Exiles Return Home

c. 515 BC
Second Temple Built

c. 4 BC
The Birth of Jesus

c. AD 30–62
Acts of the Disciples

c. AD 34
Paul Converted

c. AD 70
Second Temple Destroyed

PROPHETS — **GOSPELS** — **HISTORY** — **EPISTLES**

c. 587 BC
Solomon's Temple Destroyed and the Final Exile to Babylon

c. AD 30
Jesus's Death

The Letters

The Intertestamental Period

METANARRATIVE OF SCRIPTURE

Creation

In the beginning, God created the universe. He made the world and everything in it. He created humans in His own image to be His representatives on the earth.

Fall

The first humans, Adam and Eve, disobeyed God by eating from the fruit of the Tree of Knowledge of Good and Evil. Their disobedience impacted the whole world. The punishment for sin is death, and because of Adam's original sin, all humans are sinful and condemned to death.

Redemption

God sent His Son to become a human and redeem His people. Jesus Christ lived a sinless life but died on the cross to pay the penalty for sin. He resurrected from the dead and ascended into heaven. All who put their faith in Jesus are saved from death and freely receive the gift of eternal life.

Restoration

One day, Jesus Christ will return again and restore all that sin destroyed. He will usher in a new heaven and new earth where all who trust in Him will live eternally with glorified bodies in the presence of God.

FREE FROM SHAME

WEEK ONE

DAY 1
Introduction — What is shame?

DAY 2
Shame and the Curse

DAY 3
Shame and the Past

DAY 4
Shame and Relationships

DAY 5
Shame and Identity

WEEK ONE

SCRIPTURE MEMORY

Therefore, if anyone is in Christ, he is a new creation; the old has passed away, and see, the new has come!

2 Corinthians 5:17

WEEK ONE

♦

We must *look to God*, the only One who is completely perfect, *for a solution.*

♦

DAY ONE

Week One
Day One

Read Genesis 2:15–3:9.

Practice this week's memory verse.

INTRODUCTION: WHAT IS SHAME?

A dark cloud hangs over your head. It travels with you wherever you go. Its gloom is there when you get ready for work in the morning, reminding you of last night's mistakes. And it is there when you lie down to sleep, replaying the day's failures. It feels like the cloud is an x-ray before others—as if everyone can see your darkness within. Feeling exposed, you try to hide. You drop your head low and cower in a corner.

The picture above is an illustration of shame. Shame is the feeling of intense sadness, humiliation, or guilt in response to wrong behavior. It is much different than simply feeling embarrassed about something. Rather, shame is an overwhelming feeling that makes us feel grieved, outcast, and alone. And more than anything, shame makes us want to hide. Sometimes we experience shame because of our own sin, and sometimes we experience it due to sin committed against us. Whatever the cause of shame, it is something that all experience at one time or another. Because shame is a universal part of the human experience, it is important to know how to navigate and overcome it. But, in our own strength, we cannot solve the problem of shame. Therefore, we must look to God, the only One who is completely perfect, for a solution. He gives us His Word to show how sin and shame are linked and what He accomplished to remove both.

So this study will look to God's Word, the Bible, for the truth that sets us free from sin and shame. We will also discuss shame both through the lens of our own sin and the shame we experience due to other people's sins against us. Shame inflicted by others causes similar feelings as shame from guilty behavior does. But regardless of what type of shame we encounter, Scripture provides insight into its origin. With that in mind, during the first week of this study, we will walk through scenarios in which shame manifests and discuss how the gospel of Jesus Christ addresses these situations. Then, for weeks two and three, we will read about biblical characters who experienced shame and how God set them free from the shame of their past and pain. For the final week, we will explore some practical steps we can take to live out the freedom from shame offered to us in Christ.

The Bible indicates that the first emotional reality for humans is shamelessness. Genesis 2:25 shows this when it states, "Both the man and his wife were naked, yet felt no shame." In the beginning, God created humans in His image, ordaining them to reflect His nature and character. Adam and Eve, the first man and woman, came into existence and entered a marriage union. Because Adam and Eve were morally innocent, God put them in the garden of Eden, the place where His holy presence dwelled. There, Adam and Eve lived in the Lord's nearness and abundant grace. Their physical nakedness pointed to their spiritual nakedness. In other words, Adam and Eve had an intimate relationship with each other and with God. Their entire being was exposed, but they were unashamed because sin had not yet tainted their image. The man and woman had no fault or imperfection to hide. Instead, they openly radiated God's likeness.

However, Adam and Eve soon compromised their innocence when they disobeyed God's command not to eat from the Tree of the Knowledge of Good and Evil. One day, a serpent crept into the garden—unbeknownst to Adam, who was supposed to guard Eden. The serpent was Satan in disguise (Revelation 12:9). The snake slithered to Eve and deceived her into thinking that God was not good. Eve then acted on her desire to be her own lord. In an attempt to assert autonomy, the woman ate the tree's fruit, and her husband followed suit (Genesis 3:6). Adam and Eve sinned,

Week One
Day One

and they no longer had their original, innocent state. Sin brought them into shame, and a dark cloud formed over their heads.

Genesis 3:7 reveals how their disobedience exposed them to their nakedness. We can assume they saw not only their physical nakedness but also their spiritual nakedness. Their eyes were opened to evil, which led them to revolt against God, and they were ashamed of what they witnessed. To cover their disgrace from each other, they made clothing out of fig leaves. And to cover their disgrace from God, they hid from Him. Though Adam and Eve attempted to conceal the shame of sin, God still saw them. God saw their corruption, but because of His grace, He pursued them. God knew where they were hiding, but still, He called out to Adam, asking him, "Where are you?" God took the initiative in finding His image-bearers.

Today's passage highlights that God will come after the ashamed. He does not leave us to suffer alone under the dark cloud. As redemptive history progresses, we see how in the person of Jesus Christ, God the Son left the honor of His heavenly throne to enter the fallen world. He pursued us to the cross, where He died to save us from sin. Therefore, we can let go of our mediocre attempts to cover our corruption. And we can let the shame of personal sin and outside affliction move us to depend on the work of Jesus Christ.

> "GOD WILL COME AFTER THE ASHAMED. HE DOES NOT LEAVE US TO SUFFER ALONE UNDER THE DARK CLOUD."

WEEK ONE DAY ONE QUESTIONS

◆ In what ways do you experience shame?

◆ How do you repeat Adam and Eve's attempt to cover shame?

◆ What is your response to God's pursuit of you through Jesus Christ?

NOTES

WEEK ONE

Jesus took all of our shame to *the cross,* where He died the *death we deserved.*

DAY TWO

Week One
Day Two

Read Genesis 3:14–24.

Practice this week's memory verse.

SHAME AND THE CURSE

Have you ever felt like you were cursed? Perhaps you have avoided watching your favorite team's championship game in fear that your presence would bring them misfortune. Or maybe you have withheld best wishes to a newly married couple so that your words would not cause their relationship to end. Some of us may feel that we are cursed when we reflect on our lives and witness one bad circumstance after another. A broken home, mediocre performance in school, romantic rejection, and career setbacks unfold and make life a continuous mess. Feeling cursed can also impact our relationship with God. We may think God is against us. We may think God grimaces at us and has left us alone in the world.

Feeling cursed is not the result of spells or voodoo; instead, it is the result of shame. We view ourselves as loathsome beings. When we look in the mirror, we only see someone who is unlovable, unattractive, and uninteresting. Our downcast state reflects itself in life's disappointments. Someone may think, *Of course, my family treats me poorly. I am so stupid; I deserve it.* Shame leads us to enter a state of perpetual humiliation and disgrace over our existence. It sends us on a journey of living like we are under a curse.

Scripture exposes this reality in the curse of Genesis 3. Yesterday, we read how Adam and Eve's sin—or their disobedience to God's law—brought shame. When the Lord came to Adam, Eve, and the serpent, He listed curses that would afflict them because of their sin. Biblical curses are the consequences of sin. They serve as both God's just punishment for the guilty and the natural ramifications of choosing life outside of God's goodness. In today's reading, we learn that because of their sin, Adam and Eve will continually wrestle under a curse and experience the shame of disobedience.

God cursed Eve with painful childbirth and a difficult marriage (Genesis 3:16). God cursed Adam with back-breaking and futile work (Genesis 3:17–19). And both of them would eventually return to the dust from which they came (Genesis 3:19). The punishment for eating fruit from the forbidden tree was death, which these curses embody in the fullest sense. Also, Adam and Eve would no longer experience the pleasure and vitality of living in God's presence. The Lord banished them from the garden. Adam and Eve entered a world tainted by their sin and gave birth to a sinful humanity. Bearing the curse, they encountered struggle after struggle.

But God gave the most severe curse to the serpent. He pronounced utter defeat over Satan (Genesis 3:14–15). The serpent—the one who set out to destroy God's people—ultimately receives the Lord's contempt. In this curse, there is also a promise. Genesis 3:15 states, "I will put hostility between you and the woman, and between your offspring and her offspring. He will strike your head, and you will strike his heel." God declared that Eve would give birth to a Son who would conquer the serpent, overcoming evil and ending its schemes.

Through the promise, we see that God did not turn against Adam and Eve. He did not keep His people without His presence. His disposition was still one of loving grace. Though death was ahead for humans, God spared Adam and Eve. He sustained breath in their lungs. Adam and Eve did not die immediately but had the opportunity to participate in God's call to fruitfulness (Genesis 3:20). Furthermore, the Lord covered their shame (Genesis 3:21). God provided clothing made of animal skins. He hid them in His mercy and righteousness.

Despite the curse, there is a blessing. Though Adam and Eve would ache in a fallen world, God foreshadowed their salvation. The promise in Genesis 3:15 is called the *protoevangelium*, which means "first gospel." Here, we see a glimpse of the person and work of Jesus Christ. And, in the blood-stained animal skins that covered Adam and Eve, we see the foreshadowing of the sacrifice of the coming Savior.

Truly God, Jesus became a human, the promised Son of Eve. He bore the sin of God's people and embodied the curse (Galatians 3:13). He was rejected, mocked, and abandoned though He was perfectly righteous. Jesus took all of our shame to the cross, where He died the death we deserved. By His blood, He paid the punishment for our disobedience and clothed us in His obedience. In His life, death, and resurrection, Jesus defeated Satan. He crushed the serpent's head, casting it into eternal darkness.

Because of Christ's salvation, living under the curse is no longer our experience. We can come out of our shame, for our depravity is not beyond the realm of God's power. Jesus erased the shame of our disobedience. He freed us from perpetual humiliation and disgrace over our existence. We can have true pleasure and vitality in God's presence again. When we feel like outcasts, we can remember that Jesus left God's paradise to bring us home. When we see no one of worth when we look in the mirror, we can know that Christ's worth covers our sins. When bad things happen again and again, we can be sure that God's blessing in Jesus Christ outweighs them all.

> **BECAUSE OF CHRIST'S SALVATION, LIVING UNDER THE CURSE IS NO LONGER OUR EXPERIENCE.**

WEEK ONE
DAY TWO
QUESTIONS

◆ Read Galatians 3:10–14. What insight does this passage give to today's reading?

◆ How do the curses reveal the seriousness of sin?

◆ In what ways does the gospel help through feeling cursed?

NOTES

WEEK ONE

♦

While He does not erase our past, God does *transform* it so that our past points to *the gospel's power.*

♦

DAY THREE

Week One
Day Three

Read Acts 7:54–8:3, Acts 9:1–22, and 1 Timothy 1:12–16.

Practice this week's memory verse.

SHAME AND THE PAST

You travel to your childhood home for Christmas, anxious about reuniting with the past. As soon as you pull into the driveway, memories flood your mind. Unfortunately, these memories do not bring the warmth of nostalgia but cause your body to freeze. You open the front door. Mom is running around the kitchen while dad is buried in a newspaper—just how you left them. No one notices your presence. You fall into your old adolescent footsteps and retreat to your room. As you sit on your bed, surrounded by relics of another generation, you remember the favoritism given to your older sibling, the insults, and the loneliness. Years have gone by, and you have changed. But the shame of your past still lingers like the smell of burnt popcorn.

Experiencing shame over the past is difficult. At some point, we may all remember the hurt and harm that we caused or that was inflicted upon us. In this case, the past becomes a chain, continuously tying us down to darkness, regardless of how much time has passed or how much self-improvement we have made. But God can change this reality. When we put our faith in Jesus Christ, the Lord loosens the chains of what once was and gives us hope for what will be. While He does not erase our past, God does transform it so that our past points to the gospel's power.

We see an example of this in the life of the Apostle Paul. God transformed the sinful past of Paul's life for God's good purposes. Paul is one of the New Testament authors and was a major player in the early church movement. Scripture details how Paul's missionary efforts spread the good news of Jesus Christ throughout Asia Minor and into Europe. But Paul's past is not as exemplary. Before he became a believer, Paul, who was also known as Saul, was part of the Sanhedrin. The Sanhedrin was a council of elders who held religious authority among the Jewish people in the post-exilic period. We first see Paul in Acts 7 when Stephen, a disciple of Jesus, is on trial. Stephen is arrested because he performs many signs that convey Christ's resurrection and kingship. People lie about Stephen and accuse him of blasphemy. The Sanhedrin then interrogates Stephen, but he responds with God's Word. When Stephen claims to see Jesus standing at the right hand of God in heaven, the councilmen stone him. Scripture states that Paul approves the killing and oversees the slaughter (Acts 7:58, 8:1).

Paul's terror does not end there but continues to torment other believers. In Acts 8, persecution against the church ensues. Paul leads this campaign against Christians and imprisons many. Then, one day on the road to Damascus, Paul has an encounter with Jesus, who asks why he is persecuting believers. The glory of the Lord knocks Paul to the ground and blinds him. Days later, a disciple named Ananias is sent by the Lord to Paul. Though he is hesitant to approach the man who has committed much evil, Ananias obeys God's direction, for the Lord has chosen Paul to spread His name (Acts 9:15). God gives Paul his sight back and blesses him with the indwelling Holy Spirit, and then Ananias baptizes him.

Because of God, Paul is now the faithful believer he once opposed. And he begins preaching the message he once arrested others for preaching. The Lord uses Paul's shameful reputation to show that no sin is greater than His plans.

Paul's past informs his testimony about God's mercy in 1 Timothy 1:12–16. In his letter to Timothy, who was another early church leader, Paul acknowledges that he was a "blasphemer, a persecutor, and an arrogant man" (1 Timothy 1:13). Like all of us sinners, Paul deserved punishment for his rebellion. Paul did not have the moral ability to overcome the disgrace of his actions. On his terms, Paul would have continued to promote the kingdom of darkness. But God showed Paul mercy by uniting him to Jesus Christ, saving him from death, and forgiving all his crimes. In verse 15, Paul affirms the power of the gospel to save sinners. He claims he was the worst of all, yet he stands completely different. The fact that Paul's past is no longer his present is proof that Christ indeed conquered sin and rose from the grave. Paul's past is also evidence of God's patience with sinners. The Lord does not desire that His people perish but preserves them for eternal life through Christ. At His appointed time, God pours out His grace, and not even the most wicked person can resist.

If we trust in Jesus Christ, we can face the weight of our past without shame. We can acknowledge the awful things that happened to us in our childhood. We can acknowledge the wrongs we committed. Because of Jesus's salvation, these moments no longer serve the kingdom of darkness. They can no longer bind us. God has been merciful to us in Christ Jesus. He shielded us from judgment, and He has shown us compassion. So now, we can live freely in the present, knowing that God is using our past as a tool for His redemptive mission. We can live with expectant hope for the future, confident that God will completely shape us into the image of Jesus. When memories of the past come back to haunt us, let us remember to shine the glory of our Savior.

> "IF WE TRUST IN JESUS CHRIST, WE CAN FACE THE WEIGHT OF OUR PAST WITHOUT SHAME."

WEEK ONE
DAY THREE
QUESTIONS

◆ In what ways does your past affect you?

◆ How does the gospel of Jesus Christ speak to these areas?

◆ How can you live in a way that demonstrates the transforming power of the gospel?

Editor's note: Luke refers to Paul as Saul in Acts 7–12 and parts of chapter 13. Contrary to what some believe, Saul does not change his name to Paul after being saved. Instead, Saul and Paul are the same names; "Saul" is the Hebrew version of "Paul," which is Greek. Because Koine Greek was the language predominantly spoken across the Roman Empire at this time, Saul likely reverts to his Roman name, Paul, because he is starting his first missionary journey in 13:9. For the sake of simplicity, we only refer to Paul's Greek name in this study day.

NOTES

WEEK ONE

Through *our faith* in Jesus, shame no longer affects our *relationship* with the Lord.

DAY FOUR

Week One
Day Four

Read Genesis 3:10–13 and Psalm 69.

Practice this week's memory verse.

SHAME AND RELATIONSHIPS

Have you heard the silence of a long car ride home after your spouse embarrassed you at dinner? Have you avoided a coworker about whom you told an insensitive joke at the staff holiday party? Have you ignored your parents' phone calls after years of mounting pressure for perfection and demands to meet their expectations? Whether we experience disgrace from personal wrongdoing or outside affliction, relationships can suffer under shame. Scripture reveals shame's effect on relationships. While shame primarily leads us to a broken relationship with God, it can also lead to broken relationships with others. However, Scripture also reveals how, through His saving work, Jesus Christ reconciles us to the Father and, therefore, enables us to pursue reconciliation with others despite the harm that we, or they, caused.

Shame often creates distance and stirs up blame. Today, we revisit a portion of Genesis 3 to see how shame can affect us relationally. We come back to the story of Adam and Eve and read the conversation they had with God after He exposed their disobedience. First, in Adam and Eve's response, we see distance. Adam and Eve hid from their Maker. Instead of running to God for forgiveness, they turned from Him in fear. They did not exercise trust in God's goodness and, as a result, created a chasm between them and the only One who could help.

Because Adam and Eve forsook dependence on God, shame then produced blame. Adam said, "The woman you gave to be with me—she gave me some fruit from the tree, and I ate" (Genesis 3:12). Adam placed responsibility on Eve for his sin, though God specifically commanded him to not eat from the Tree of the Knowledge of Good and Evil. The disgrace of falling short of God's law led Adam to avoid seeing his moral inability.

Furthermore, Adam also placed blame on God in this verse. Adam recognized Eve as the woman that the Lord gave. In this way, Adam seemed to think that the problem was with God. Adam likely believed that God gave him an unsuitable companion who was the reason for the mishap. Eve then blamed the serpent. She said, "The serpent deceived me, and I ate" (Genesis 3:13). Though Satan's deception was true, Eve left out the part where she twisted the Lord's words and decided for herself that the tree's fruit was good to eat (Genesis 3:2, 6).

By blaming other parties, Adam and Eve mistakenly assumed they were victims. So they neglected to repent and humble themselves before God. But, in this attempt to avoid shame, they crawled deeper into its hole. Their relationship with God and each other fractured. Still, God planned reconciliation through the coming Savior.

A firm relationship with the Lord helps us endure shame from others. We see this truth in David's Psalm 69. David is a well-known king and songwriter from the Old Testament. In this psalm, David described the insults he received because of his faith in the Lord. He stated, "For I have endured insults because of you, and shame has covered my face. I have become a stranger to my brothers and a foreigner to my mother's sons because zeal for your house has consumed me, and the insults of those who insult you have fallen on me" (Psalm 69:7–9). In addition to his family, the people of the city mocked David. He begged God to rescue him from despair.

However, in the midst of his pain, David also put his trust in the Lord's character. In verse 13, he said, "But as for me, Lord, my prayer to you is for a time of favor. In your abundant, faithful love, God, answer me with your sure salvation." David knew the Lord would not compromise His promises. In this way, David exercised faith in the Lord's salvation. David believed the coming Savior would make a bridge between God and His people so that they could escape the shame of sin and rest in the Lord's presence.

Though David sought reconciliation with the Father through the coming Savior, he did not seek reconciliation for his enemies. In verses 22–28, David prayed for God to curse those who shame the faithful. In this psalm, we do not see David praying for his enemies to repent and know God. Nevertheless, David's prayer points to the greater prayer of Jesus Christ, who was shamed to the utmost and still sought reconciliation for those who crucified Him (Sproul, 910).

As the perfect Son of God, Jesus had a pure zeal for the Father. Jesus was devoted to the Father and loved doing His will. But people despised His faithfulness. He was falsely accused and convicted. He was beaten on the way to the cross and was mocked as He hung there. But, though He was unjustly treated, Jesus did not curse His enemies. Instead, He asked the Father to forgive them (Luke 23:34). Furthermore, Jesus saw us, who were still enemies of God; He loved us despite our rebellion and wanted to restore our relationship with the Father (Romans 5:7–8). Fulfilling Psalm 69:21, Jesus was offered gall to alleviate the pain and sour wine for His thirst. At this sign, Jesus claimed the punishment for sin was finished, and He took our sin and shame to the grave.

Like Adam and Eve, we had a broken relationship with the Lord. Because of our shame, we assumed God was not safe, blamed Him for the wrong in our lives, and put distance between us and His love. As a result, we had broken relationships with others, failing to take responsibility for our actions and seeing those around us as the problem. Like David, we have been gifted with faith in Jesus and have reconciliation with God through Him. But maybe we still struggle with letting our restored relationship with God inform our relationship with those who have shamed us.

Through our faith in Jesus, shame no longer affects our relationship with the Lord. Therefore, we can accept responsibility for and repent of our lingering sins, knowing that God does not condemn us and is working to change us. We can let the comfort of this truth lead us to reconcile with others. Because Christ is our retreat from the shaming words of our spouses, coworkers, or parents, we can pray that they would receive forgiveness through Jesus. And we can respond to their insults and mocking with compassion, knowing that we are patterning after our Savior.

WEEK ONE DAY FOUR QUESTIONS

◆ What verse(s) in Psalm 69 stick out to you?

◆ What insight does David's prayer give when you are feeling ashamed?

◆ Read 2 Corinthians 5:11–21. How can this passage help you restore relationships with others?

NOTES

SCRIPTURES FOR FACING FORGIVENESS

2 Corinthians 5:18–21

Everything is from God, who has reconciled us to himself through Christ and has given us the ministry of reconciliation. That is, in Christ, God was reconciling the world to himself, not counting their trespasses against them, and he has committed the message of reconciliation to us.

Therefore, we are ambassadors for Christ, since God is making his appeal through us. We plead on Christ's behalf, "Be reconciled to God." He made the one who did not know sin to be sin for us, so that in him we might become the righteousness of God.

Colossians 1:19–22

For God was pleased to have all his fullness dwell in him, and through him to reconcile everything to himself, whether things on earth or things in heaven, by making peace through his blood, shed on the cross.

Once you were alienated and hostile in your minds as expressed in your evil actions. But now he has reconciled you by his physical body through his death, to present you holy, faultless, and blameless before him.

Romans 5:10–11

For if, while we were enemies, we were reconciled to God through the death of his Son, then how much more, having been reconciled, will we be saved by his life. And not only that, but we also boast in God through our Lord Jesus Christ, through whom we have now received this reconciliation.

Colossians 3:12–13

Therefore, as God's chosen ones, holy and dearly loved, put on compassion, kindness, humility, gentleness, and patience, bearing with one another and forgiving one another if anyone has a grievance against another. Just as the Lord has forgiven you, so you are also to forgive.

Write a journal entry that identifies an outside source of shame. Perhaps your shame stems from a boss who belittled you, a parent who ignored you, or a loved one who rejected you. Consider how the sting of this relationship has impacted your sense of self. Invite Jesus to remedy the hurt and point you to His salvation. Then, meditate on how Christ's work to forgive you of your sin liberates you to forgive others.

WEEK ONE

Jesus, through His saving work, gives us *eyes to see* His image in ourselves.

DAY FIVE

Read Genesis 1:26–27, Psalm 139:13–15, Ephesians 2:3–5, and 2 Corinthians 5:17.

Practice this week's memory verse.

SHAME AND IDENTITY

Loser. Failure. Filthy. Unlovable. Burdensome. When we experience shame over our identity, we may imagine these titles tattooed across our foreheads. In these moments, shame becomes more than a response to actions we did or actions that were done to us—it becomes a response to who we are. As a result, our confidence in who God made us to be weakens. Even after putting our faith in Jesus, we may struggle with considering ourselves "bad Christians" as we fall behind on Bible study reading, forget to pray, or feel spiritually dry for a season. Shame over our identity tries to send us back into the shadows, but Jesus, through His saving work, gives us eyes to see His image in ourselves. Jesus erases the disgraced titles from our foreheads and helps us radiate God's design with confidence.

Shame over identity derives from sin's distortion of image-bearers. *Imago Dei* is a Latin phrase meaning "image of God." This phrase communicates a theological concept echoed in Genesis 1:26–27. In these verses, we see the Father, Son, and Holy Spirit gather and agree to make unique creatures: humans. God says, "'Let us make man in our image, according to our likeness. They will rule the fish of the sea, the birds of the sky, the livestock, the whole earth, and the creatures that crawl on the earth.' So God created man in his own image; he created him in the image of

God; he created them male and female" (Genesis 1:26–27). The Lord forms humans in His likeness. In other words, though cloaked in flesh and bones, humans are spiritual beings and reflect God's love, justice, wisdom, compassion, patience, etc. God graciously shares some of His characteristics, called communicable attributes, with us. As a result, we hold inherent dignity, worth, and authority.

However, this dignity, worth, and authority were compromised at humanity's fall in Genesis 3. Sin attached itself to human nature, making us sinners. The shame of disobedience began to define us. Paul explains this truth in Ephesians 2:3, which states, "We too all previously lived among them in our fleshly desires, carrying out the inclinations of our flesh and thoughts, and we were by nature children under wrath as the others were also." This verse identifies that in our own nature, we belong to wickedness. Rebellion corrupts our identity, and evil likes to remind us of this reality. The voice of Satan, that old serpent that slithered into the garden, reminds us of our guilt. His accusations are sometimes louder than God's truth. Then, we dwell on and perpetuate brokenness: our malice, injustice, foolishness, apathy, impatience, etc. And we run from our Designer, the only One who can remedy our image. But fortunately, God neither leaves His people ignorant of who they were created to be nor leaves them without the path to wholeness.

As we see in Psalm 139, the psalmist David knows wholeness is found in the Lord and praises God for His design. David sings, "For it was you who created my inward parts; you knit me together in my mother's womb. I will praise you because I have been remarkably and wondrously made. Your works are wondrous, and I know this very well" (Psalm 139:13–14). David remarks on how his life—not only his physical being but also his spiritual redemption—is the result of the Father's work. This realization moves David to worship and to draw near to the Lord. David stands confidently in His Maker, despite the fact that David is a broken image-bearer. The shame of sin is heavy on David's life, but, at the same time, David sees himself as God's remarkable and wonderful creation.

How is David able to have such a high view of himself when he committed so much disgrace? After all, his sin included crimes as grievous as sexual assault and murder (2 Samuel 11), and his children, too, were responsible for similar sins. But, because of his forward faith in the Savior, David was given the righteousness of Jesus Christ. The summary of David's life includes a heart to please the Lord, genuine repentance, and clinging to God for salvation. Therefore, the king is able to celebrate his identity in Psalm 139 because he knows it rests securely in the Lord's hand.

Jesus Christ came to save us from sin, and through His salvation, Jesus restored our identity. Jesus clothed us in His dignity, worth, and authority. His image became ours, and God wrapped us in His delight. By His Spirit, Jesus shed the scales from our eyes so that we could believe in Him and in His power. This power changed us from being rebellious children of wrath to righteous children of God. This power gave us life (Ephesians 2:5). Second Corinthians 5:17 states, "Therefore, if anyone is in Christ, he is a new creation; the old has passed away, and see, the new has come!" Through our faith in His salvation, we are no longer what we once were. Sin no longer defines us. Jesus transformed us into redeemed image-bearers, so we can see who God made us to be in Christ and celebrate His design. We can walk in this identity with confidence, knowing that the Holy Spirit will help us pursue a fuller reflection of God's image until His work is complete.

> "JESUS CHRIST CAME TO SAVE US FROM SIN, AND THROUGH HIS SALVATION, JESUS RESTORED OUR IDENTITY."

WEEK ONE
DAY FIVE
QUESTIONS

◆ How do your sins define you? How does the gospel impact those definitions?

◆ Use Psalm 139:13–15 to write a prayer to the Lord.

NOTES

END-OF-WEEK REFLECTION

Think back on all of the Scripture that you read and studied this week as you answer the questions below.

What did you observe about God and His character?

What did you learn about the condition of mankind and yourself?

How does this week's Scripture point to the gospel?

Week One
Day Five

How do the truths you have learned this week about God, man, and the gospel give you hope, peace, or encouragement?

How should you respond to what you read and learned this week? Write down one or two specific action steps you can take this week to apply what you learned. Then, write a prayer in response to your study of God's Word.

WEEK ONE APPLICATION QUESTIONS

Before we begin a new week of study, take some time to apply and share the truths of Scripture you learned this week. Here are a few ideas of how you could do this:

- Schedule a meet-up with a friend to share what you are learning from God's Word.

- Use these prompts to journal or pray through what God is revealing to you through your study of His Word.

Lord, I feel…

Lord, You are…

Lord, forgive me for…

Lord, help me with…

- Spend time worshiping God in a way that is meaningful to you, whether that is taking a walk in nature, painting, drawing, singing, etc.

- Paraphrase the Scripture you read this week.

- Use a study Bible or commentary to help you answer questions that came up as you read this week's Scripture.

- Take steps to fulfill the action steps you listed on Day 5.

- Use highlighters to mark the places you see the metanarrative of Scripture in one or more of the passages of Scripture that you read this week. (See *The Metanarrative of Scripture* on page 14.)

FREE FROM SHAME

WEEK TWO

DAY 1
Hagar: Rejected to Received

DAY 2
Hannah: Distressed to Rejoicing

DAY 3
Gomer: Unfaithful to Restored

DAY 4
Woman with the Issue of Blood: Sick to Healed

DAY 5
Woman at the Well: Condemned to Redeemed

WEEK TWO

SCRIPTURE MEMORY

Jesus said, "Everyone who drinks from this water will get thirsty again. But whoever drinks from the water that I will give him will never get thirsty again. In fact, the water I will give him will become a well of water springing up in him for eternal life."

John 4:13-14

WEEK TWO

Our *rejection* **and shame should send us to** *the feet of Jesus.*

DAY ONE

Read Genesis 16.

Practice this week's memory verse.

HAGAR: REJECTED TO RECEIVED

From the time we are young children until we are old and gray, we all share one of the same fears—rejection. Whether you are the most confident person in the room or the one who has the lowest self-esteem, rejection brings us all to the same painful level. Rejection from parents, friends, a significant other, or even our jobs leads us down a path of deep shame. We are ashamed that we do not measure up to the expectations of others. We are ashamed that we seem to be lacking in some way or assume that there must be something wrong with us. And we feel the deep sting of lost love and respect.

Sin has a way of making us both the perpetrator and the victim as we inflict shame on others and endure it ourselves. In Genesis 16, we see this clearly displayed in the lives of Sarai and Hagar. Abram and Sarai had been in the land of Canaan for ten years. God had promised that He would give them a child, and yet, Sarai was still barren. Sarai likely felt great shame over her barrenness. Women around her were having children and establishing their families for generations, and she was unable to perform the simple mandate God gave in the garden of Eden to be fruitful and multiply (Genesis 1:28). Sadly, her shame over her own situation led her to a poor solution and ill-treatment of another person. Our human plans always have consequences when we ignore God's divine plan. Sarai dealt with her shame by looking inward for a solution instead of trusting God's promise.

Sarai's solution was Hagar, an Egyptian servant in her household. Sarai's impatience led her to give Hagar to Abram in order to produce a child. During this period in history, it was culturally common for men to take their servants as wives. But it was contrary to God's perfect design for marriage between one man and one woman (Genesis 2:23–24). Taking matters into her own hands would prove to be destructive in many ways to Sarai and her family. Hagar conceived Abram's child, whom they named Ishmael, and Sarai mistreated Hagar, despite the fact it was her plan. In this difficult situation, Hagar now felt the sting of rejection simply because she was able to do something her mistress could not. Her misery and shame drove her to the wilderness. It was there that she surprisingly encountered hope and encouragement.

By running into the wilderness, it is possible that Hagar was attempting to return home to Egypt. But instead, she found solace in a divine visitor. The angel of the Lord met Hagar by a spring and asked her, "where have you come from and where are you going?" (Genesis 16:8). It seems important to note that Hagar only answered the first question. She was running from her mistress, but she likely felt lost and confused in her next steps. Like Hagar, shame leaves us feeling alone in a wilderness of pain, dejection, and hopelessness, wondering where to turn next. Yet the angel of the Lord provided hope for Hagar and for believers as we are reminded of God's love and character through the remaining events in this narrative.

The angel of the Lord told Hagar to return to her "mistress and submit to her authority" (Genesis 16:9). This was probably not what Hagar wanted to hear. Why would she return to the person who rejected her, mistreated her, and caused her great shame? However, God did not leave Hagar without hope in this command.

We first see glimmers of hope through the use of names. Ishmael's name means "God hears." Hagar's son would be a daily reminder that God heard Hagar in her pain and shame. Hagar's response to the Lord was to name Him El-Roi, "the God who sees." In her darkest hour, Hagar acknowledged that it was the Lord alone who saw her desperation and shame. It was the Lord who provided comfort and blessing. Lastly, the angel of the Lord followed up the difficult command with a blessing. Hagar's son would be the father of his own great nation. Hagar returned to her mistress, likely uncertain of her treatment but filled with hope from the promise of the Lord. Hagar's obedience to the Lord's command shows that she trusted in the God who saw and heard her.

The feelings of rejection and shame have the same effects today as they did in Sarai and Hagar's time. When we try to handle these emotions on our own, we end up like Sarai and Hagar, either inflicting pain or running away. Yet our rejection and shame should send us to the feet of Jesus. Only in His loving arms will we find rest and comfort for the pain we feel.

We can also find rest and comfort in what Jesus did for us on the cross. Jesus faced unthinkable shame as He bore our sin on the cross. He understands us and sympathizes with us and provides hope in our weakest moments. Because of Christ's perfect sacrifice, Hebrews 4:16 encourages us to "approach the throne of grace with boldness, so that we may receive mercy and find grace to help us in time of need." When the pain of rejection overwhelms your heart, remember: God sees you, and He hears you. For those in Christ, we have moved from rejected to received. Through Christ, we can leave the wilderness in victory and rest in His promise of the future.

> **WHEN THE PAIN OF REJECTION OVERWHELMS YOUR HEART, REMEMBER: GOD SEES YOU, AND HE HEARS YOU.**

WEEK TWO
DAY ONE
QUESTIONS

- In what ways do shame and rejection drive us to do sinful things we know are not in the Lord's plan?

- How do you see God's sovereignty at work in this narrative? Now read Genesis 21:8–21 and Genesis 25:12–18. How did God fulfill His promise to Hagar and Ishmael?

- The angel of the Lord asked Hagar, "where have you come from and where are you going?" (Genesis 16:8). What shame or rejection has led you into the wilderness in a past or present season? How does the love and hope of the God who sees you and hears you enable you to walk in victory?

NOTES

WEEK TWO

God *alone* brings
healing and comfort.

DAY TWO

Week Two
Day Two

Read 1 Samuel 1–2.

Practice this week's memory verse.

HANNAH: DISTRESSED TO REJOICING

At some point in our lives, we all experience the distress that comes from a broken heart. Whether it is from a bad breakup, infertility, the loss of a loved one, or the end of a career we love, our hearts break for the deep pain and void this disappointment brings. Sadly, this loss can also lead us to a place of shame as we think we no longer measure up to a standard the world has defined. We deem ourselves as "less than" because we have failed in some capacity. We long to rejoice once again—to feel valued, accepted, loved, and remembered. This theme occurs not only in our lives today but in the lives of people like Hannah in the Old Testament. Her life is an example that though we may be brokenhearted and distressed, the Lord is near, and He remembers us.

Hannah lived during the final period of the judges. She and her husband, Elkanah, would travel to Shiloh each year to sacrifice to the Lord at the tabernacle, which had resided in Shiloh since Joshua and the Israelites had conquered the Promised Land. Elkanah loved Hannah dearly, but Hannah was barren. As was customary in that era, Elkanah likely took a second wife to bear him children. His second wife's name was Peninnah, and Scripture tells us she would taunt Hannah "severely just to provoke her" (1 Samuel 1:6). It is important to pause here and note that Elkanah having two wives does not serve as an indication that bigamy was God's original intent for marriage. Genesis 2:24 is clear that God's design for marriage was for it to be between one man and one woman; however, God still worked through Hannah's situation. In 1 Samuel, we see the shame and failure Hannah felt over her barrenness and the taunting of her rival that made her weep and kept her from eating. Elkanah attempted to help Hannah in her pain. He showed his love for her by giving her double portions of food and even asking if his love for her was not better than sons (1 Samuel 1:8). But his comfort was not what Hannah needed most.

Our shame over our inabilities can bring us to our knees in agony and defeat. Hannah found herself in this dark place, yet she chose to get up from her place of defeat and go to the Lord in prayer. In this way, Hannah provides us with an example that nothing this world offers will ease the shame and pain we feel. God alone brings healing and comfort. In Hannah's prayer, she called God the "Lord of Armies." It is here in 1 Samuel this term is first used in Scripture (1 Samuel 1:3, 11). This name for God was Hannah's acknowledgment that God is all-powerful and sovereign over the situation she faced. Hannah asked the Lord to remember her and give her a son, whom she promised to give to the Lord to work in His service. Hannah was willing to give up the very thing she longed for the most in order to serve the Lord.

As Hannah prayed silently before the Lord, Eli, the priest, thought she was drunk. But Hannah told Eli that she was praying to the Lord out of her anguish and resentment. Shame often leads us to this same place. We feel great anguish over our failures while simultaneously experiencing resentment over our situation, other people's treatment of us, and even the Lord for leaving us in such a dark place. But Hannah shows us what to do with that anguish and resentment—take it to the Lord.

When Hannah left her time of prayer, Scripture tells us in 1 Samuel 1:18, "Hannah went on her way; she ate and she no longer looked despondent." Her husband had attempted to console her through food and his love, but Hannah's deep emotional needs were only satisfied in the Lord. No amount of human consolation can ease our pain and shame. Only the Lord can bring true comfort and peace as He did for Hannah. Hannah left joyfully that day—not because she had been granted a child at that moment but because she had been with the Lord.

God did indeed bless Hannah with a child, and Samuel was born to her sometime later. As was the custom of that day, children were not weaned until they were two or three. At that time, Hannah took Samuel and presented him to the Lord for service. Many mothers would have been sad and downcast as they left their child, but Hannah joyfully prayed to the Lord, rejoicing in His salvation and holiness. She praised Him for His sovereignty over the earth and her life.

Broken hearts, shame, anguish, and resentment are all products of the Fall and sin. And while they may be painful, God uses them for His purposes and His glory. We must remember that it was the Lord who kept Hannah from conceiving (1 Samuel 1:5). And though it brought her pain, when He opened her womb in His timing, it was for His glory and to further His plan of redemption. God's purpose for our life is to bring Him glory. We will face many earthly trials that lead to broken hearts and the shame, anguish, and resentment that likely accompany them. But God redeems all things. The prophet Isaiah reminds us of this truth when he writes in Isaiah 43:1, "Do not fear, for I have redeemed you; I have called you by your name; you are mine." We are not forgotten in our pain. We know this is true because God sent Jesus to heal our broken hearts and restore us to our Father. We may experience distress for a time, but when we go to Him, we will experience great joy.

> **GOD'S PURPOSE FOR OUR LIFE IS TO BRING HIM GLORY.**

WEEK TWO DAY TWO QUESTIONS

◆ How have you experienced both anguish and resentment in a season of shame? How did the Lord provide comfort in those moments and help you not to respond in a sinful way?

◆ Read Psalm 34:18 and Psalm 147:3. In this study day, we discussed how brokenheartedness can sometimes lead to shame. How do these verses provide encouragement for seasons of brokenheartedness and shame?

◆ Take a moment to read through Hannah's prayer again, and notice how she praises the Lord from beginning to end. In the space provided, write out your own prayer of praise for who God is and how He has redeemed you and healed your broken heart. Alternatively, if you have not experienced healing, pour out your heart to God, and ask for comfort and healing.

NOTES

WEEK TWO

We need not feel shame, for God provides valuable discipline and beautiful restoration *in Christ.*

DAY THREE

Week Two
Day Three

Read Hosea 1–3.

Practice this week's memory verse.

GOMER: UNFAITHFUL TO RESTORED

Many prophets in Scripture were asked to live out difficult situations to proclaim a message of repentance and judgment to God's chosen people. One of these difficult situations was the real-life depiction of unfaithfulness by the prophet Hosea's wife. God used Hosea's life as a living picture of Israel's unfaithfulness by calling Hosea to marry a woman named Gomer, whom many scholars believe was a prostitute. And Hosea was not only called to marry her — when Gomer repeatedly went to be with other men, Hosea was called to buy her back and restore her. By the end of today's study, we will see how Hosea's message to Israel, illustrated through his relationship with Gomer, still has implications for our lives today. Though we follow Jesus, we are often unfaithful; however, we need not feel shame, for God provides valuable discipline and beautiful restoration in Christ.

God called Hosea to be a prophet during a pivotal time in the history of Israel. At the time of his calling, Israel had been split into the northern and southern kingdoms for some time. Hosea's prophetic message was to the northern kingdom of Israel. Israel had one bad king after another, and each one led the people to serve other gods and follow the pagan practices of the surrounding nations. It was amid this dark and crooked generation that God asked Hosea to depict both His love and discipline for this adulterous nation. God did this by asking Hosea to marry Gomer, "a woman of promiscuity," and have children with her (Hosea 1:2). Through Hosea, God would show how He was faithful to the Israelites despite their unfaithfulness to Him. God would also use Hosea to warn the Israelites about the consequences of their unfaithfulness.

One way that God warned the Israelites was through the names of Hosea and Gomer's children. Hosea and Gomer named their first son Jezreel, which meant "God sows." This name reminded the people of the city where Jehu killed the remaining family of the evil King Ahab, thus eliminating his line on the throne (2 Kings 9–10). Jezreel also pointed to the coming judgment upon Israel and the destruction of Jehu's royal line by a future invader. Then, Gomer bore Hosea's daughter, named Lo-ruhamah, which meant "no compassion." God no longer had compassion on Israel and her evil ways. Hosea's final child was a son named Lo-ammi. Simply translated, his name meant "not my people." One of the saddest verses in Hosea is 1:9, when God speaks through the prophet and says, "for you are not my people, and I will not be your God." Hosea's children were meant to remind this rebellious nation that their sin was grievous to their holy God, and their sin had consequences.

The meaning of these names builds as Hosea 2 goes on to describe the continual sin and unfaithfulness of Israel. Gomer's repeated adultery serves as the allegory for this description. And while this should have had great meaning for the Israelites, they still turned a blind eye to their sin. Their unfaithfulness led them into ruin, destruction, and exile. But as we see in the remainder of chapter 2 and chapter 3, God provides restoration. Just as Hosea bought Gomer back, God would buy His people back with the blood of His Son. We, too, are recipients of this gift of forgiveness and restoration.

The narrative of Hosea has so much for us to learn today. In our fallen and sinful state, we are just like an unfaithful, adulterous woman to our faithful God. At every turn, we shirk His love and seek the pleasures of this world. But we are not left there, as Ephesians 2:4–5a explains, "But God, who is rich in mercy, because of his great love that he had for us, made us alive with Christ even though we were dead in trespasses." This verse shows that just as Hosea paid a price for Gomer, God paid a price for us. The blood of Christ now covers us and restores us. But sin is still present in the world. Though redeemed by Christ, we still struggle with sin and unfaithfulness. The guilt and shame we feel over repeated sin can oftentimes crush us and make us ineffective for the Lord. When tempted to despair over past or present sin, we have to remind ourselves of what Paul says in Romans 8:1, "Therefore, there is now no condemnation for those in Christ Jesus." We walk in victory because Jesus paid the penalty. We can seek repentance and walk victoriously with our Savior.

Hosea's message also reminds us that there are consequences for our sin. Though we are redeemed, we still make poor, sinful decisions that can have earthly repercussions. The Israelites had to experience the Lord's discipline in order to correct their rebellious behavior, and so do we. God is a loving Father who desires the best for His children, and so He corrects us. As the author of Hebrews says in Hebrews 12:11, "No discipline seems enjoyable at the time, but painful. Later on, however, it yields the peaceful fruit of righteousness to those who have been trained by it." God's discipline is for our good and helps us grow in holiness. It is not meant to shame us but to refine us and draw us closer to Him. And though it might be difficult and painful, this beautiful relationship with our Father will be a testimony to our hearts—and to the world—of just how great He is!

Though the first part of Hosea shows the consequences of sin, God's love and sovereignty are still on display in Hosea. In chapter 1, we read about the names of Hosea's children and the sad reality they represented. By the end of chapter 2, the Lord redeems these names. As children grafted into the promises of God through Christ, these names now represent all God will do for us. God has shown us compassion in Christ, and one day we will live in the eternal land He has sown for us. It is there, in the new heaven and the new earth, that He will be our God, and we will be His people (Revelation 21:1–3).

WEEK TWO
DAY THREE
QUESTIONS

◆ In what ways is Hosea's message just as relevant today? How do you see the gospel displayed in these chapters?

◆ What sin continuously causes you to stumble and be unfaithful to the Lord? Instead of living in shame, how can you seek repentance and walk in victory with Jesus?

◆ Using the chart on pages 10–11, what attributes of God do you see displayed in these chapters of Hosea? How does the knowledge of God's character help you grow in faithfulness and holiness?

NOTES

WEEK TWO

The *blood of Jesus* makes us healed and *whole.*

DAY FOUR

Read Mark 5:21–34 and Leviticus 15:19–30.

Practice this week's memory verse.

WOMAN WITH THE ISSUE OF BLOOD: SICK TO HEALED

Have you ever felt like an outcast? At some point in our lives, those feelings of rejection, worthlessness, and lack of belonging creep in. We feel ashamed because we suddenly feel like we do not belong or fit the societal norms in which we live. This can leave us feeling isolated, sad, and desperate. In our passage today, the woman who approached Jesus likely felt all these things while living as an outcast in her own culture. But her faith in the One who heals brought restoration through Jesus.

As we read Mark 5:21–34, we see one miracle take place as Jesus is on His way to another miracle. Jesus arrives on the shore of the Sea of Galilee, and Jairus, a synagogue leader, approaches Him. His daughter is dying, and he asks Jesus to come and heal her. Jesus does not hesitate and follows the man immediately, with a large crowd following behind Him. And while Jesus does go on to heal Jairus's daughter (Mark 5:35–43), He first stops to address a woman, also in need of healing, who has been bleeding for twelve years. We do not know specifically what caused the bleeding, but we know she spent all her money on doctors and was still not healed. Among her fellow Jews, she was considered an outcast. This large crowd that followed Jesus presented her with an opportunity to blend in and seek the help she so desperately needed.

In order to fully understand this situation and the desperation that this woman likely felt in Mark 5, we have to return to the Old Testament. In Leviticus 15:19–30, we read about the rules women had to follow when they had their monthly menstruation cycle or when they bled outside of their typical menstruation cycle. They were considered unclean for seven days. Anything they touched or sat on was considered unclean as well. If another person touched them, that person was considered unclean. Women were not considered ceremonially clean until seven days after the bleeding stopped. Additionally, in the case of bleeding outside of a woman's typical cycle, she was then also required to take a sin offering to the priest.

This particular woman had dealt with a bleeding disorder for twelve long years. Imagine the physical, spiritual, and emotional turmoil this caused. She was always considered unclean. She had to make sure people knew she was near so that she would not touch someone and accidentally make them unclean. And because of her uncleanness, she was not allowed to enter the court of women at the temple. She lived a life of separation, both physically and spiritually. She lived among people but not as a truly welcomed and embraced member of society.

This woman saw Jesus in the crowd and likely realized He represented the hope and healing she so desperately craved. Faith sprouted in her heart, and though she possibly touched others and could be called out for what she was doing, she took that first small step of faith toward Jesus. She reached out and grabbed the hem of His robe and immediately felt the healing power of the Lord. Jesus knew He had been touched, and healing power left Him. But instead of being made unclean by the touch of this woman, He imparted His perfect love, which made her healed. Jesus could have let her go without speaking to her, but He had a greater plan.

Jesus asked who touched Him, and this woman was given the opportunity to confess her faith before the Lord. Then Jesus, calling her "daughter," acknowledged her inclusion into a new family. She was no longer a spiritual outcast, and Jesus's confirmation of her healing ended her separation from society physically. This woman could walk away from her encounter with Jesus with her head held high and her heart joyful and healed. Imagine how full her heart was as she walked away from an encounter with the Savior of the world. Her shame was gone, for Jesus had replaced it with abundant life (John 10:10).

Like this woman, we too long to be healed and whole, but sin has made us all shame-filled outcasts. Adam and Eve were forced from the garden of Eden because sin had no place in the presence of our holy God. And from that time forward, mankind has remained as outcasts from the presence of God. For thousands of years, mankind's hearts longed to be healed, whole, and living in His presence, but sin brought separation. However, just as Jesus healed this woman, Jesus healed the hearts of mankind through His sacrifice on the cross.

Those who come to Jesus and seek forgiveness and healing for their sinful hearts will no longer be outcasts. Jesus returns believers to the presence of God. We no longer endure separation due to our unclean hearts; we are now heirs with Christ (Romans 8:17). Jesus also gives us a new spiritual family for eternity. The blood of Jesus makes us healed and whole. He destroys the sin and shame in our hearts and bids us to "go in peace" (Mark 5:34). We belong to the Savior of the world, and there is no safer or more loving place to be.

> **WE BELONG TO THE SAVIOR OF THE WORLD, AND THERE IS NO SAFER OR MORE LOVING PLACE TO BE.**

WEEK TWO
DAY FOUR
QUESTIONS

What can you learn from the faith of this woman who suffered for twelve years? How was her shame turned into something beautiful?

Are you desperate for Jesus like this woman in Mark 5? When life is hard and it seems like there is no way out, how can you take action to seek Jesus and His wisdom first?

In what ways have you felt like an outcast in life? How has Jesus healed you, made you whole, and given you a new family of faith?

NOTES

WEEK TWO

♦

The *living water* Jesus offers cleanses hearts from sin and sets us *free from shame* and condemnation.

♦

DAY FIVE

Week Two
Day Five

Read John 4:1–30 and 39–42.

Practice this week's memory verse.

WOMAN AT THE WELL: CONDEMNED TO REDEEMED

Many of us likely have childhood memories of playing outside in the sweltering heat of the summer months. Whether at a beach, a lake, a park, or in our own backyards, we played hard and inevitably became thirsty. Upon realizing our great thirst, there was nothing quite like that first cool drink of water to quench our dry mouths. As we grow and mature, we quickly realize that it is not just our mouths that become parched, but our souls do as well. Our sinful hearts crave the living water only Jesus can provide. In John 4, Jesus shares this living water with a Samaritan woman, whose redeemed heart leads her to tell others about Jesus so that they, too, can receive the living water He provides.

In order to share living water with this Samaritan woman, Jesus met her right where she lived. In his recounting of these events, the Apostle John provides us with important locations, times, and cultural facts to display Jesus's sovereignty and intentionality in this situation. The Samaritans were disliked by both the Jews and the Gentiles. After the northern kingdom of Israel fell to the Assyrians in c. 722 BC, the exiled and displaced Jews intermarried with the Gentiles of surrounding nations. This intermarriage was considered an abomination by the Jewish people in Jerusalem and created animosity between both Jews and Samaritans. The Jews despised the Samaritans so much that they often took a longer route to Galilee from Jerusalem rather than the quicker path through Samaria. But on this day, Jesus intentionally traveled the road to Samaria.

Jesus and the disciples arrived in the city of Sychar around noon. This time is important because it helps us note that it was in the heat of the day. Most women went to the well early in the morning or late in the evening to avoid the heat. This woman's visit to the well at noon was likely to hide from the judgmental and prying eyes of other women. But on this day, her visit was divine. While the disciples entered the city to buy food, Jesus asked this woman for a drink. The Samaritan woman was shocked for two reasons. First, she was a woman. Women were not treated with great respect in this period and were rarely spoken to in public by men. Second, Jesus was a Jew. This woman knew the cultural differences and hatred between her people and the Jews (John 4:9). But in His usual pattern, Jesus cast aside cultural norms and cared for the heart of this woman.

Her heart needed the living water only Jesus provides. The idea of living water was confusing yet appealing to this woman. As she sought to understand what Jesus meant, she first thought this living water would be a means to no longer come to the well where her sin and shame were exposed to her neighbors. This water would be a way to avoid their judgmental stares and comments. But Jesus was calling her to more. He did not just want her to avoid others, but instead, He wanted to give her an abundant life through Him. As Jesus exposed her sin, she quickly realized Jesus is no mere man. Here, at a well in Samaria, Jesus revealed Himself as the Messiah to this woman. Though Jesus is Jewish and came to save His people first, He joyfully offers salvation to all. The living water Jesus offers cleanses hearts from sin and sets us free from shame and condemnation. This living water is eternal and meant to be shared with others.

Scripture tells us the living water that fills and quenches our souls is the Holy Spirit. In John 7:37–39, Jesus stands before a crowd in Jerusalem and says, "'If anyone is thirsty, let him come to me and drink. The one who believes in me, as the Scripture has said, will have streams of living water flow from deep within him.' He said this about the Spirit." When we seek Jesus for the forgiveness of our sin, He does not leave us to fend for ourselves after we are saved—He provides the Holy Spirit, who fills our hearts. The Holy Spirit seals us, convicts us, guides us in truth, intercedes on our behalf, and enables us to bear fruit for the kingdom (Ephesians 1:13; John 16:8, 13; Romans 8:26–27; Galatians 5:22–25). When we are filled with the Spirit, our hearts seek to serve Christ because they are changed and made new.

The Samaritan woman was changed after her encounter with Christ. She walked away from the well refreshed and satisfied because she received the living water Jesus offered her. Her response was no longer to cower in shame but to share about this experience with others as she went to the town and testified about the Messiah. When the gospel changes our hearts, we are compelled to share the good news of Christ with others. Jesus makes our hearts whole. We no longer bear the weight of condemnation but stand before the Lord, righteous and redeemed.

As the living water overflows from our redeemed hearts, we joyfully take the gospel to our parched and dying world. Like Jesus, we intentionally meet people where they are and share the living water that changed our life and destroyed our sin and shame. In Psalm 34:8, the psalmist reminds us of the joy found in Christ when he says, "Taste and see that the Lord is good. How happy is the person who takes refuge in him!" Jesus provided refuge for the Samaritan woman, and her joy-filled soul shared the gospel with those who likely judged her life. Jesus provides refuge for us as well, and because we have tasted the living water, we proclaim the gospel without fear. We proclaim the Savior of the world.

WEEK TWO
DAY FIVE
QUESTIONS

◆ How does the narrative of the Samaritan woman teach us about Christ and His intentionality to provide living water to all who seek Him? What cultural barriers did He reject in order to share the gospel?

◆ How have others condemned you for your sin? How have you condemned yourself? How has the living water of Christ cleansed and healed your heart from sin, shame, and condemnation?

NOTES

END-OF-WEEK REFLECTION

Think back on all of the Scripture that you read and studied this week as you answer the questions below.

What did you observe about God and His character?

What did you learn about the condition of mankind and yourself?

How does this week's Scripture point to the gospel?

Week Two
Day Five

How do the truths you have learned this week about God, man, and the gospel give you hope, peace, or encouragement?

How should you respond to what you read and learned this week? Write down one or two specific action steps you can take this week to apply what you learned. Then, write a prayer in response to your study of God's Word.

IMAGE-BEARERS ONCE MORE

When God created mankind, He made us in His image. We see this first in Genesis 1:26–27, when God said, "Let us make man in our image, according to our likeness. They will rule the fish of the sea, the birds of the sky, the livestock, the whole earth, and the creatures that crawl on the earth.' So God created man in his own image; he created them in the image of God; he created them male and female." And even after the Fall, when we first experienced sin and shame, we still reflected His image. This truth is apparent in Genesis 9:6 when God creates His covenant with Noah after the flood and still refers to man as being made in His likeness.

However, even though we were made in God's image, we had not yet received the image of God through Christ. Now, because of Christ's work on the cross, we can receive His image and therefore become a new creation in Christ.

In the diagram on page 93, you will see text boxes on the left that are filled with verses that tell us who we were before receiving Christ. The text boxes on the right display who we are called to be after receiving Christ and how the joy of our salvation destroys shame. When sin creeps in and shame overwhelms you, remember that God saved you through Christ. Remember Romans 12:1, which says, "Therefore, brothers and sisters, in view of the mercies of God, I urge you to present your bodies as a living sacrifice, holy and pleasing to God; this is your true worship." May we no longer experience shame from our pain and past; rather, may we worship God and display Him to the world.

Galatians 2:2

I have been crucified with Christ, and I no longer live, but Christ lives in me. The life I now live in the body, I live by faith in the Son of God, who loved me and gave himself for me.

Romans 7:23–24	Romans 12:2
Mark 7:21–23	Hebrews 10:21–23
Philippians 3:18–19	Philippians 3:20–21
Isaiah 59:2–3a	Psalm 16:8, 11
Isaiah 59:7–8	Hebrews 12:12–14

WEEK TWO APPLICATION QUESTIONS

Before we begin a new week of study, take some time to apply and share the truths of Scripture you learned this week. Here are a few ideas of how you could do this:

- Schedule a meet-up with a friend to share what you are learning from God's Word.

- Use these prompts to journal or pray through what God is revealing to you through your study of His Word.

Lord, I feel…

Lord, You are…

Lord, forgive me for…

Lord, help me with…

Week Two
Days Six + Seven

- Spend time worshiping God in a way that is meaningful to you, whether that is taking a walk in nature, painting, drawing, singing, etc.

- Paraphrase the Scripture you read this week.

- Use a study Bible or commentary to help you answer questions that came up as you read this week's Scripture.

- Take steps to fulfill the action steps you listed on Day 5.

- Use highlighters to mark the places you see the metanarrative of Scripture in one or more of the passages of Scripture that you read this week. (See *The Metanarrative of Scripture* on page 14.)

FREE FROM SHAME

WEEK THREE

DAY 1
Zacchaeus: Outcast to Accepted

DAY 2
A Man Born Blind: Blamed to Freed

DAY 3
Peter: Wayward to Commissioned

DAY 4
Paul: Self-Righteous to Humble

DAY 5
Jesus: Bore Our Shame

WEEK THREE

SCRIPTURE MEMORY

More than that, I also consider everything to be a loss in view of the surpassing value of knowing Christ Jesus my Lord. Because of him I have suffered the loss of all things and consider them as dung, so that I may gain Christ

Philippians 3:8

WEEK THREE

Following Jesus does not mean you are *perfect*; **it means you are broken and realize your** *need for a Savior.*

DAY ONE

Week Three
Day One

Read Luke 19:1–10 and 5:30–31.

Practice this week's memory verse.

ZACCHAEUS: OUTCAST TO ACCEPTED

Your arms ache, but you are almost there. One last pull and you will be at the top of the tree with a clear view of the street below. The wind blows through your hair as you lean out of the tree to look around. Inhaling sharply, you watch Jesus walk closer. Your heart races. Will He notice you in the tree? Has He already been told who you are and what everyone thinks of you? A man like that could never be around a person like you. Then someone cries out your name.

Zacchaeus wanted to see Jesus, but he was too small. So he climbed a tree to see Him. Zacchaeus likely did not expect Jesus to stop and talk with him. As a chief tax collector, we can assume Zacchaeus was rich, powerful, and alone. Tax collectors worked for the much-hated Roman Empire, which conquered the Jews. The Jewish population of the day viewed tax collectors as traitors who sold their morals to get rich. Many also suspected tax collectors of overcharging and pocketing the extra money for themselves. As the chief of collectors, Zacchaeus was viewed as the worst of the worst. The people of Jericho probably steered clear of such a terrible, sinful man. Zacchaeus was despised and shamed by society for his sins.

Yet Jesus did not view Zacchaeus the way the world did. The world expected Jesus to walk by a man like him—one too small and worthless to merit attention. However, Jesus defied expectations and not only noticed Zacchaeus but called him by name. Jesus knew exactly who Zacchaeus was and wanted to be with him.

After calling Zacchaeus to His side, Jesus told him that He would stay at Zacchaeus's house. This was a great honor. Having dinner with a person symbolized trust and friendship with that person. Jesus was essentially telling the watching world that Zacchaeus, and people like him, are His friends and worthy of His attention.

However, the text shows that those around Zacchaeus did not understand why Jesus would want to stay with him. In Luke 19:7, we read that all those who saw this interaction "began to complain, 'He's gone to stay with a sinful man.'" Jesus eventually explained that He had come for the lost, but before this, we witness a beautiful depiction of how Jesus transforms people.

After Jesus invited Zacchaeus into an intimate friendship, knowing the type of person Zacchaeus was, Zacchaeus climbed out of the tree and joyfully accepted Jesus's invitation (Luke 19:6). Then, we see how Jesus's presence changed Zacchaeus's heart. Instead of wanting to cheat people, we see a generous man. Zacchaeus's transformation is evident in verse 8 when Zacchaeus says, "Look, I'll give half of my possessions to the poor, Lord. And if I have extorted anything from anyone, I'll pay back four times as much." Zacchaeus is not trying to impress Jesus; rather, he is changed because Jesus has brought him into a relationship with Himself.

Like Zacchaeus, you may have family or friends who have rejected you because of past actions. Perhaps someone has caught you stealing, under-reporting your income, or cheating on a test. Maybe you have heard someone say, "I'm ashamed of you." You may even feel like a social outcast at times. However, Jesus came into this world to be with people just like you. He does not see you the way the world sees you. He is not ashamed of you. Instead, He wants to be with you.

In fact, Jesus wants to be with you so much that not long after His dinner with Zacchaeus, Jesus died on a cross to take away our sin and shame. Dying on the cross to save us was, after all, why He came to earth. The Apostle Paul explains this truth in 1 Timothy 1:15 when he writes, "This saying is trustworthy and deserving of full acceptance: 'Christ Jesus came into the world to save sinners'—and I am the worst of them." Jesus did not leave heaven and come to earth in order to hang out with the self-righteous and proud. In actuality, He often distanced Himself from those groups and ran toward the lonely, the shamed, and the rejected (Luke 19:10). Following Jesus does not mean you are perfect; it means you are broken and realize your need for a Savior.

Jesus is not ashamed of you—even though you may have done terrible things and others may have shamed you. Instead of shaming you, Jesus calls you into a relationship with Himself. We can listen to this call through Scripture and the Holy Spirit. And, if we obey Him, we will find the truest, deepest friendship, full of love and grace, from a God who loves us so much that He died to bear our shame.

> "INSTEAD OF SHAMING YOU, JESUS CALLS YOU INTO A RELATIONSHIP WITH HIMSELF."

WEEK THREE
DAY ONE
QUESTIONS

◆ Imagine yourself in a tree like Zacchaeus. List out the things that you often feel shamed for.

◆ Imagine that Jesus calls out your name as you sit in the tree. What do you feel? How do you react?

◆ Fill in the chart with the type of people the world values versus the type of people with whom Jesus spent His time. For help with this chart, look up the following passages: Luke 7, Luke 10:38–42, and John 18:10.

Who the World Values	Who Jesus Spent Time With
• *"Good" people*	• *Zacchaeus*

NOTES

WEEK THREE

♦

Things we view as *limitations* **God can use to show the world** *His strength.*

♦

DAY TWO

Read John 9:1–11.

Practice this week's memory verse.

A MAN BORN BLIND: BLAMED TO FREED

Many of us have at least one trait we wish we could change. Maybe you struggle to speak in public or are incredibly shy. Maybe you tend to say the first thing that comes to your mind and often wish you could hold your tongue more. Perhaps you weigh more or less than you think you should, so you dress a certain way to hide your weight. Sometimes, we cling to traits either out of shame or obsession. And because of this, one trait can become the basis of our entire identity.

The man in John 9:1–11 is known for only one trait—blindness. We never learn his name, his hobbies, or his personality. He is identified only by his disability. In this society, all physical disabilities were seen as the consequence of sin. If you, like this man, were born with a disability, then society believed it was either your sin or your parents' sin that caused it. This is why the disciples ask whose fault it is that this man is blind.

The source of heartache in this man's life is not that he is blind—it is that people only see him as blind. This characteristic determines the course of his entire existence. Because he is blind, he is likely left out of many sectors of society. From the disciples' questions, we can imagine that he may have been labeled as a sinner and outcast. Why? For being born a certain way.

Jesus offers a new perspective on the cause of his blindness. Jesus says it is not the man's sin or his parents' sin that led to his blindness; instead, it is "so that God's works might be displayed in him" (verse 3). Sometimes, we face obstacles in life that are the direct result of our own sin or the sin of another. Other times, there are obstacles in our path that have nothing to do with sin and everything to do with God's glory. The world viewed this man's blindness as a hindrance, but God transformed it into a gift, which makes his blindness both beautiful and worthwhile. This man, unlike many, is likely very aware of his need for a Savior. After all, he spends his days begging for the charity of others to survive. He knows that he cannot make it on his own.

Unlike those of us who strive to control our lives and become our own saviors, this man understands he needs help. When Jesus strangely rubs spit and dirt into this man's eyes, he lets Jesus do it. He obeys and washes off the mud from his eyes in order to see. His blindness reveals his need for Jesus, and he immediately obeys his Savior's voice when he hears it. What the world deems a curse, God uses as a blessing so that this man can be saved.

Further, God uses the blindness of this man to reveal Himself to others. The whole town sees the love and power of Jesus through this man; millions of others over thousands of years have also seen God's power and love through his story recorded in Scripture. Jesus uses this man to bring others to faith. Things we view as limitations, God can use to show the world His strength.

The body, mind, and soul that you have are gifts from a good God. Too often, we are ashamed of the way we look or embarrassed of our limitations that require another's help. The world tells us that beauty means perfection and strength means independence, and we believe it. Yet God looks at us and sees Himself. We are made in His image to reflect His glory (Genesis 1:26–27). As we studied on Week 1 Day 5, King David understood this truth when he wrote this beautiful prayer to God: "For it was you who created my inward parts; you knit me together in my mother's womb. I will praise you because I have been remarkably and wondrously made. Your works are wondrous, and I know this very well. My bones were not hidden from you when I was made in secret, when I was formed in the depths of the earth" (Psalm 139:13–15).

Because of the Fall, our bodies are limited. However, these limitations do not need to be a source of shame but instead a reminder that we need a Savior. The Apostle Paul knew this and said of his own weakness, "I will most gladly boast all the more about my weaknesses, so that Christ's power may reside in me. So I take pleasure in weaknesses, insults, hardships, persecutions, and in difficulties, for the sake of Christ. For when I am weak, then I am strong" (2 Corinthians 12:9b–10). So, if you have ever felt like the world only sees you one way or that you are tossed aside because of the way you were born, remember that God does not see you the way the world does. We may be tempted to ask, *Why was I made this way?* But instead, let us wonder, *How will God use this limitation for His good?*

> "
> THE BODY, MIND, AND SOUL THAT YOU HAVE ARE GIFTS FROM A GOOD GOD.
> "

WEEK THREE
DAY TWO
QUESTIONS

◆ Read 2 Corinthians 12:6–10. How did Paul view his weaknesses?

◆ Think about a limitation you have that might have caused you shame in the past (e.g., needing rest and thus being unable to get everything done in a day). How could God use that limitation for His good?

◆ Write a prayer, thanking God for the body you have been given — even with its limitations. Take some time to pray that God would use your limitations for His good.

NOTES

WEEK THREE

Jesus died on the cross precisely for people like Peter: *sinners.*

DAY THREE

Read John 18:15–18, 25–27, John 21:15–19, and Acts 4:5–13.

Practice this week's memory verse.

PETER: WAYWARD TO COMMISSIONED

Most of us desire to be fully known and fully loved by someone. Yet many of us believe that if others knew the worst parts about us, they would certainly run away. So we hide our shameful moments and flaws from the world, allowing the humiliation to dwell in our souls. This feeling is not unique to us; it was likely shared by the Apostle Peter. As we read Peter's story in Scripture, we come to realize that Peter, too, had his fair share of embarrassing memories. He constantly made rash decisions that he later came to regret. For example:

- *One of Peter's most famous scenes in the Bible is when Jesus walks on water. Boldly and quickly, Peter asks Jesus to allow him to walk on water, too. Jesus calls him, and Peter steps out of the boat. But immediately, he becomes fearful and nearly drowns as a result (Matthew 14:22–33).*

- *Jesus accuses Peter of being an agent of Satan in one instance because Peter speaks too quickly without realizing the meaning of his words (Matthew 16:23).*

- *Three times, Jesus asks Peter to stay up and pray with Him on the night before His death. This is the moment when Jesus wants Peter's assistance most of all, yet Peter falls asleep all three times rather than staying up to pray (Matthew 26:36–46).*

- *Peter boldly promises Jesus that he will never betray Him, but three times in a row, he denies knowing Jesus after He is arrested. When Peter speaks his third denial, Jesus looks right at him, and Peter breaks down into tears (Luke 22:61–62).*

Jesus knows everything about Peter and sees him at his worst moments. Peter cannot hide his most shameful memories from Jesus because Jesus is his Creator and the all-knowing God. And yet, Jesus never abandons Peter. After Peter's denial, Jesus dies on the cross and is resurrected three days later. Then, He finds Peter doing exactly what he had been doing at their first meeting: fishing.

However, despite Peter's unfaithfulness, Jesus never changes His mind about Peter. Jesus died on the cross precisely for people like Peter: sinners. Jesus sacrificed Himself on the cross so that His betrayers could be forgiven and find restoration. In response to Peter's failed attempts to pray and his three denials, Jesus reminds Peter three times of the life to which He has called him. The man who no one would choose as a leader is chosen by God to grow and encourage the Church (John 21:15–19).

After this final encounter with Jesus, Peter is a new man, all because Jesus forgives him and calls him to a life of purpose. This allows Peter to exchange his guilt for glory and trade in fear for boldness. Later in life, Peter will proudly go to jail rather than deny Jesus again (Acts 4). Eventually, as church tradition tells us, Peter even dies the same death on the cross as Jesus did, a final act of boldness to advance the kingdom of God.

Jesus knows everything about us. He sees our best and also our worst moments. There is no hiding our shame from Him. But the things about us that we are most ashamed of do not have to hold us back from being who God created us to be. Before anyone else could, Jesus saw the potential for Peter to be a leader of the Church because that is what God made Peter to do. Jesus has a purpose for you, and nothing you do or nothing that has been done to you will change His mind.

If you want to live a life with Jesus—a life marked with purpose and growing God's kingdom—you can. You do not need to hide your sins from Him. Indeed, you cannot. Instead, you give up your old self and allow Him to replace it with a new one (Ephesians 4:22–24). Jesus sees your potential, even if no one else does, because He made you to glorify Him and enjoy Him forever. And nothing in this world can take that away.

> "IF YOU WANT TO LIVE A LIFE WITH JESUS—A LIFE MARKED WITH PURPOSE AND GROWING GOD'S KINGDOM—YOU CAN."

WEEK THREE
DAY THREE
QUESTIONS

- Imagine that you are talking with Jesus, as Peter did in John 21, and Jesus asks you, "Do you love me?" What would your answer be to Jesus?

- List the things in your life that make you feel unworthy of living a life for God. Confess those things to God, and ask Him to wash away those sins in your life.

- Read 1 Peter 2:9. What characteristics do followers of Jesus have, according to Peter?

NOTES

WEEK THREE

God does not see you the way the *world* does.

DAY FOUR

Week Three
Day Four

Read Isaiah 64:6 and Philippians 3:2–9.

Practice this week's memory verse.

PAUL: SELF-RIGHTEOUS TO HUMBLE

Shame often pours out of our hearts as we despair in our real or perceived failures, but it can also creep into our lives from the boasting of others. For instance, you may feel like a good parent until a friend brags that their child is already accomplishing tasks that your child has not even tried yet. You might think you excel at school until a friend confides that she has a 4.0 GPA and casually mentions that if others do not, they must not be trying very hard. You might be proud of your body until you overhear another person in the gym locker room saying they have only 5% body fat because they take their health seriously, unlike others. As others voice pride in themselves, we drown in shame.

You might remember the Apostle Paul from week one of this study (refer to Acts 9:1–22). He possessed a laundry list of attributes he could boast about within his culture. He was:

- *A Roman citizen, which came with certain privileges and opportunities that were denied to non-citizens;*
- *A Pharisee who followed God's laws from the Old Testament (and more) better than anyone else;*

- *A student of Gamaliel, who was a highly respected rabbi at the time;*
- *A zealous advocate for God who persecuted Christians before he himself encountered Christ.*

Paul had all the qualifications to be a highly respected member of society—a man who others wanted to be, a man who many people probably compared themselves to, only to find they were lacking. Most of us dream of being so well respected in society. Yet, Paul says that none of these things matter to him anymore. All of his accomplishments and toil to keep the Law perfectly are now useless trash compared to what he gains in Christ. How can this be?

Paul understands that all of his good deeds and accolades are nothing compared to the love of Jesus. We so often try to earn the love of God or others through doing good things. Isaiah tells us that all of those "good works" are as helpful for our salvation as an old rag (Isaiah 64:6). The world says Paul is good because of his work and bloodline, but Jesus says Paul is good because of grace. It is not Paul's family line, education, citizenship, friend group, or actions that save him; it is the work of Jesus dying on the cross to pay for Paul's sins. Because of this, Paul no longer wants to boast about his accomplishments but instead wants to boast about his Savior. Paul's perspective can be a helpful reminder if you compare yourself with others who seem to have more to offer God than you do. You can remember that God does not see you the way the world does. The world puts all of us in a line, ranking us by how much we contribute. God places us behind the cross so that He sees only the blood of Jesus.

Many of the New Testament Epistles are written by Paul. Throughout these letters, Paul mentions his weaknesses as opportunities to boast about God's strength and denounces his achievements as worthless. This was a rare characteristic in Paul's day, just as it is in ours. We consume social media, where people constantly put forward their best days and hide their worst. They show us how much they accomplish but not how often they fail. We, too, might be guilty of this. The more we boast in ourselves, the less room there is to boast in God. As we brag about ourselves, we steal God's glory and give others the false impression that we are responsible for the good things in our life rather than giving thanks to a Father who blesses His children. And as we do so, we might be causing shame in others rather than revealing the grace of Jesus.

It is important to remember that God does not love us because of our résumé or the things that we do. He loves us because of who He is. Scripture tells us that He is "a compassionate and gracious God, slow to anger and abounding in faithful love in truth, maintaining faithful love to a thousand generations, forgiving iniquity, rebellion, and sin" (Exodus 34:6–7). And in Christ, He has freely given His love, making it accessible and available to all who believe in Him. There is no number of good things you can do to earn God's love because it is already freely given—a gift of grace. Let us then not find success or failure in the things we do but in the God who draws us near.

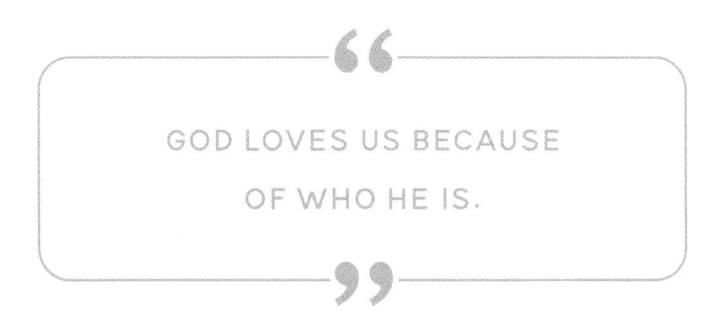

> **GOD LOVES US BECAUSE OF WHO HE IS.**

WEEK THREE DAY FOUR QUESTIONS

- Have you ever been hurt by another's self-righteous boasting?

- Are there areas in your life that you boast in rather than boasting in the Lord's provision (e.g., your children, success at work, physical health, etc.)?

- Read Psalm 34:2. How does your life (and the lives of those around you) shift when you boast in God rather than yourself?

NOTES

WEEK THREE

The *failure* in the garden of Eden is replaced by the *fulfillment* of God's promises in the garden of Gethsemane.

DAY FIVE

Week Three
Day Five

Read John 18–19 and Hebrews 12:2.

Practice this week's memory verse.

JESUS: BORE OUR SHAME

Even with His vision blurred by tears, He can see the two paths leading out of the garden. One would take Him to the Judean wilderness, where David escaped the unjust persecution of Saul. The other will take Him to certain death at the hands of His enemies. He prays for an escape but knows He will leave this garden tied up and under arrest. Hearing muffled voices, He stands, ready for the moment the world has been groaning for since the beginning.

It all started in a garden. Adam and Eve ate the forbidden fruit, ushering sin into the world. Ashamed, they attempted to cover themselves with fig leaves and hide from God. They had to leave the garden of Eden and face a fallen world. Thousands of years later, Jesus is in a garden, having confronted every temptation yet never choosing sin. Innocent and free of shame, He runs to God and follows His plan faithfully. He chooses to leave the garden and faces a fallen world about to be redeemed. The failure in the garden of Eden is replaced by the fulfillment of God's promises in the garden of Gethsemane.

Jesus is the only person with no burden of sin to carry. The rest of us feel the weight of our shame—we carry it around with us wherever we go. It creates guilt in us as we attempt to sleep, fear as we try something new, and pain as we see its effects on our relationships, especially with God. The moment Jesus chooses to stay in the garden for His arrest rather than flee, however, He faces an abundance of shame. The guards arrest Jesus at night, armed with weapons, as if He is a dangerous criminal and not an innocent man.

The King of all kings suffers the humiliation of wearing a crown of thorns and dying below a sign that mockingly reads, "The King of the Jews." The One who clothes the fields with flowers is stripped of His garments and watches as they are gambled away. The man who commits no sin is hung between two thieves to suffer a punishment only the worst of Roman criminals endure, and He watches His friends deny and betray Him in His hour of greatest need.

Even after death, Jesus's burial is quick and quiet since the ones who bury Him are afraid to be known as His followers (John 19:38–39). Unlike most of us, Jesus bears all this shame by choice. He knows exactly what awaits Him as He prays in the garden. He already told His friends at the Last Supper that He was going to die, and His prayers to His Father are so full of anguish about what is about to happen that He actually sweats drops of blood (Luke 22:44). At His trial, Jesus refuses to answer questions or defend Himself against false charges because He knows He must endure the cross. Jesus chooses to face the humiliation of an unjust trial and a criminal's death. All of this shame is heavy and humiliating, and Jesus despises it so deeply that He commits Himself to defeat it. Jesus will not allow shame to thwart His mission to rescue us.

Following in the footsteps of Adam and Eve, all of us sin (Romans 3:23) and deserve the punishment for that sin—death (Romans 6:23). The only way for us to have life again is for a substitute to die in our place. Jesus offers Himself as the perfect sacrifice to pay the price we owe. Paul confirms this truth in 2 Corinthians 5:21 when he writes, "He made the one who did not know sin to be sin for us, so that in him we might become the righteousness of God." Jesus, a pure white lamb, covers Himself in the putrid filth of our sin and dies with our shame upon His shoulders. That burden is far worse than the humiliation Jesus already suffered—it weighs more than the mocking, the gambling, the thorns, or the treason of friends. The burden Jesus feels on the cross is the full weight of sin. Every shameful thought, word, and act of ours is put on Jesus in one moment. He picks them up and carries them until His last breath. It is a death He does not deserve and shame He does not earn. Bearing this load, He frees us from all that sin ruined. The shame that weighs us down is lifted so that we can look up from the ground and into the heavens.

Turning our attention back to Jesus, we see that, three days after His death, Jesus is once again alive. Sin and death are defeated, and shame no longer has power. Jesus's death and resurrection offer a path toward freedom from the guilt and shame we all feel. Our sin is already paid for, and our shame has already been buried away in a tomb. Jesus put on your shame so that when God looks at you, He sees the pure love of the cross. If you have yet to trust in Jesus, you can choose to accept the gift of the cross at any time. It is bought and paid for, waiting for you to open. If you are a follower of Jesus, remember this gift. When the weight of shame tries to attach itself, fix your mind on the cross and picture Jesus wearing your shame like a coat. Jesus bore our shame, and because of that, we can live free from shame.

> "JESUS'S DEATH AND RESURRECTION OFFER A PATH TOWARD FREEDOM FROM THE GUILT AND SHAME WE ALL FEEL."

**WEEK THREE
DAY FIVE** # QUESTIONS

◆ How can you fight feelings of shame with the truth of the cross?

◆ Write a prayer to God, confessing where you still feel stuck in guilt. Ask Him to free you today and help you walk in that freedom.

NOTES

END-OF-WEEK REFLECTION

Think back on all of the Scripture that you read and studied this week as you answer the questions below.

What did you observe about God and His character?

What did you learn about the condition of mankind and yourself?

How does this week's Scripture point to the gospel?

How do the truths you have learned this week about God, man, and the gospel give you hope, peace, or encouragement?

How should you respond to what you read and learned this week? Write down one or two specific action steps you can take this week to apply what you learned. Then, write a prayer in response to your study of God's Word.

SHAME IN JESUS'S FAMILY

Just as Jesus chose to bear our shame on the cross, God chose to place in the family line of Jesus people who the world looked on as shameful and guilty of sin. Jesus died so that we, too, can be a part of His family, no matter what guilt or shame we carry with us. There is no sin that bars any of us from entry into the family of God. Read Matthew 1:1–17 to see the genealogy of Jesus, and then read about several members of Jesus's family with sordid pasts that God used for His redemptive plan.

Tamar
Genesis 38

Tamar is twice widowed because of both her first and second husband's sins. She is also neglected by her second husband, who prevents her from having children. Without a husband or son, she has no income or protection. Her potential third husband is kept away from her by her deceitful father-in-law. The sins of others place Tamar in a difficult position over which she seemingly has no control. After posing as a prostitute, Tamar becomes pregnant by her father-in-law, Judah, who attempts to have her killed. When Judah realizes that he is the father of Tamar's child, he confesses his sin of refusing to give his third son to her in marriage. One of Tamar's sons, Perez, continues the family line that leads to Jesus.

Rahab
Joshua 2

Rahab is a prostitute and a Canaanite. Her job and her ethnicity are looked down on by the Israelites. But, because she believes in the Lord, she lies in order to protect two Israelite spies from her own people. Because of her faith in the Lord, she asks to be spared from God's people as they attack her city, Jericho. And the Israelites do indeed spare her when they capture Jericho. Her son Boaz will go on to marry a woman named Ruth, who will continue the family line that leads to the Messiah.

Ruth
Ruth 1–4

Ruth is a Moabitess—a foreigner in Israel. As a widow and an outsider, she is an outcast in her society. Yet she is faithful to her family, hard-working, protective, and bold as she seeks out a husband to provide for herself and her mother-in-law, Naomi. Her courage eventually results in her marriage to Boaz. Together they have a son named Obed, whose grandson will be the greatest king in Israel's history, David.

Bathsheba
2 Samuel 11:1–12:25

Rather than going to war with his army, King David stays at home and falls into temptation as he sees Bathsheba, a married woman, bathing on her rooftop. David takes advantage of Bathsheba, and then Bathsheba watches powerlessly as David sends her husband, Uriah, to the front lines of battle, where he dies. Eventually, she has a son, Solomon, whom the Lord loves (2 Samuel 12:24). Solomon will be a great king over Israel and continue the family line to the Savior.

Ahaz
2 Kings 16

After the rule of King David's son Solomon, the kingdom of Israel splits into two. While David's descendants continue to rule over the southern kingdom of Judah, many turn away from the Lord. These kings commit evil acts that lead to their own downfall and the ruin of their people. One such king is Ahaz. His evil deeds include sacrificing his own son to a false god, taking treasure from the temple to use as a bribe, and teaming up with enemies of God to try to protect the kingdom rather than trusting in the Lord's protection. Bad leadership affects an entire kingdom, and Judah is led astray during the reign of Ahaz and similarly evil kings. However, God still brings His people back to His side, forgiving their iniquities. And through these men, the Savior of all mankind will come.

WEEK THREE APPLICATION QUESTIONS

Before we begin a new week of study, take some time to apply and share the truths of Scripture you learned this week. Here are a few ideas of how you could do this:

- Schedule a meet-up with a friend to share what you are learning from God's Word.

- Use these prompts to journal or pray through what God is revealing to you through your study of His Word.

Lord, I feel…

Lord, You are…

Lord, forgive me for…

Lord, help me with…

Week Three
Days Six + Seven

- Spend time worshiping God in a way that is meaningful to you, whether that is taking a walk in nature, painting, drawing, singing, etc.

- Paraphrase the Scripture you read this week.

- Use a study Bible or commentary to help you answer questions that came up as you read this week's Scripture.

- Take steps to fulfill the action steps you listed on Day 5.

- Use highlighters to mark the places you see the metanarrative of Scripture in one or more of the passages of Scripture that you read this week. (See *The Metanarrative of Scripture* on page 14.)

FREE FROM SHAME

WEEK FOUR

DAY 1
God's Promises in Christ for the Ashamed

DAY 2
Fighting Thoughts of Shame

DAY 3
Resting in the Work of Christ

DAY 4
Receiving the Grace of God

DAY 5
Hope for Shame

WEEK FOUR

SCRIPTURE MEMORY

Therefore, there is now no condemnation for those in Christ Jesus, because the law of the Spirit of life in Christ Jesus has set you free from the law of sin and death.

Romans 8:1-2

WEEK FOUR

Through His *grace* **and** *forgiveness,* **Jesus heals the wounds of our shame.**

◆

DAY ONE

Week Four
Day One

Read Isaiah 61:1–7.

Practice this week's memory verse.

GOD'S PROMISES IN CHRIST FOR THE ASHAMED

Experiencing shame can feel like being in a land of desolation. Everything around you feels joyless and lifeless. Weightiness presses down upon you. Grief pierces your heart and brings you to your knees. Shame can also feel like a prison. The shackles of shame tightly grip your ankles, and it seems as if they will never be released from you.

These feelings of desolation and imprisonment were feelings the Israelites experienced because of their exile. The consequences of their sin and wayward worship caused their land to be destroyed, and they were taken away from their home by enemies. And while many Israelites were unrepentant, the prophet Isaiah details some who acknowledged their sin. They likely felt ashamed for the ways they turned away from the Lord and led themselves to ruin. But God, in His mercy and faithfulness, did not plan to leave His people ruined and imprisoned. Although there would be judgment upon the wicked, God promised to save a remnant who would return to their land and be restored. God also promised an anointed king who would usher in this restoration and bring lasting peace and prosperity to the people. While God's promises in Isaiah 61:1–7 were partially fulfilled through Israel's restoration, these promises were ultimately fulfilled through Christ.

Jesus is the Anointed One who fulfills these promises through His death and resurrection. In fact, Jesus read these verses aloud in Luke 4:16–20, designating Himself as both the fulfillment and the fulfiller of these promises. While Isaiah 61:1–7 speaks to the Israelites' situation, these verses also speak to our own sinful condition. Whether we realize it or not, we are all in a state of mourning because we are dead in our sins. We are held captive by sin and desperately need freedom. And while many people simply ignore their sin, others of us find ourselves ashamed of our sins. Perhaps we feel the weight of our waywardness and our disobedience to the Lord. Or maybe we feel the sting of shame for how we have been sinned against. Whatever the source of our shame, this is why we need the reminder of these promises. Though we feel overwhelmed by shame, Jesus brings us healing, freedom, comfort, and transformation.

Isaiah 61:1 tells us how Jesus heals the brokenhearted. Through His grace and forgiveness, Jesus heals the wounds of our shame. His grace washes away our sin and makes our hearts new. He also gives us liberty and freedom (Isaiah 61:1). Jesus removes the shackles of our shame, releasing us from shame's grip on our lives. Though thoughts and feelings of shame may still wash over us, because of the forgiveness of Christ, we are not held captive by our shame. Jesus is the only One who can bring us true freedom from shame. Jesus also comforts us in our mourning (Isaiah 61:2). In our places of grief and despair, Jesus comes near to bring us His lasting comfort.

But Jesus also takes us out of our places of mourning. In Isaiah 61:3, we read about the beautiful transformation we receive through Christ. In place of our ashes, we receive a crown of beauty. In place of our mourning, we receive festive oil of celebration. In place of our garments of grief, we receive clothes of righteousness. In place of our shame and disgrace, we receive blessing and abundance. All of these blessings and promises are given to us through the work of Jesus on the cross. Jesus forgives our shame, transforms our lives, and makes our hearts new.

These promises may leave us to wonder, *What do these promises mean for our shame?* If Jesus sets us free from sin and shame, then we are no longer bound by it. We can walk in freedom, knowing that the circumstances of our shame do not hold us captive. If Jesus comforts us in our mourning, then we are comforted in every instance we experience shame. Therefore, we can come to Christ with our shame and receive the grace and comfort He provides. And if Jesus gives us transformation, then we no longer live in our shame. Our shame is no longer our identity — instead, our identities are rooted in the new life we have in Christ.

If we are in Christ, we do not have to act as if we live in a land of desolation. We do not have to feel as if we are imprisoned in our shame. We do not need to grieve over our shame but can celebrate because our shame is removed. We do not live with eternal shame but eternal joy because of Jesus. Therefore, let us live as those who have been set free. Let us lift our voices in gratitude and praise to Jesus, who changes our lives. Jesus is the One who takes our situations of shame and transforms them into havens of hope.

> JESUS IS THE ONE WHO TAKES OUR SITUATIONS OF SHAME AND TRANSFORMS THEM INTO HAVENS OF HOPE.

WEEK FOUR
DAY ONE
QUESTIONS

- Which one of these promises resonates with you the most and why?

- How can you rest in these promises when shame arises?

- What should your response be to these promises? How do they impact your relationship with Christ?

NOTES

WEEK FOUR

We fight **thoughts of shame by resting in the truth of the** *gospel.*

DAY TWO

Week Four
Day Two

Read Romans 8:1–4.

Practice this week's memory verse.

FIGHTING THOUGHTS OF SHAME

How could you do this? What is wrong with you? You are dirty and worthless. These are but a few of many thoughts of shame that may enter your mind. Thoughts of shame involve thoughts of condemnation. You might think thoughts—or hear others speak words—that condemn you for what you have done or what others have done to you. Thoughts of shame can feel like millions of arrows that pierce you, opening back up the wound of situations that have brought you pain. Yet, you are not helpless in this agonizing fight. You do not have to succumb to thoughts of shame when they occur or lay defeated by their power. We fight thoughts of shame by resting in the truth of the gospel.

Though our thoughts of shame seek to condemn us, the gospel declares that there is no condemnation for those who are in Christ (Romans 8:1). Why? Because Jesus has already paid the price for our sin and shame. We all stand condemned because of our sin and our failure to obey God as we should, but Christ has taken our punishment upon Himself on the cross. Therefore, we are not condemned for our sin, for our sin has been condemned through the sacrifice of Christ (Romans 8:3). The grace and forgiveness of Jesus set us free from sin and shame. Our guilt has been traded for innocence because of the blood of Christ.

If we are in Christ, we are redeemed. This means that our sins do not hold us captive any longer. We are not condemned for our sin, and we will never be condemned for our sin. However, we will still experience thoughts of shame on this side of eternity. We have a sinful flesh that thinks thoughts that are hurtful and condemning, and we have a real enemy who seeks to shame us for the sins we have committed or the sins others have committed against us. But the good news of the gospel meets us in this difficult struggle and redeems our past and pain.

First, the gospel reminds us of God's grace for our sins. Because our sins have been paid for by Christ, God will never punish or ridicule us for our sin. He will never bring up something we have done to use it against us. This truth comforts our hearts because it teaches us that thoughts of shame never come from the Lord. Whenever a shameful thought crosses our minds, we can know that thought is not from the voice of God. God's voice is different. His voice declares that we are forgiven no matter what we have done or what has been done to us. Therefore, we do not have to feel as if God is angry with us for our sins. There is no condemnation in Christ, only grace.

Second, the gospel reminds us that we walk in freedom. Romans 8:4 teaches us that if we are in Christ, we do not walk according to the flesh but according to the Spirit. Before we come to faith in Christ, our bodies are governed by our sin. We essentially walk as prisoners, enslaved to sin and headed toward an eternal punishment of death. But when Christ saves us through His sacrifice and by the power of the Spirit, our lives are transformed. We are no longer governed by sin but by grace. We walk as freed people instead of captives. The Holy Spirit given to us through Christ enables us to continue to embrace the freedom we have been given. Second Corinthians 3:17 tells us, "Where the Spirit of the Lord is, there is freedom." Because the Spirit indwells us, we experience lasting freedom. Therefore, we do not have to live as though we are still held captive by our sin and shame. As we rest in Christ's grace and walk by the Spirit, we live in the freedom Christ has bestowed upon us.

Because the gospel helps us in our struggles with shame, we can actively fight thoughts of shame with the truth of the gospel. When thoughts like *How could you do this?* or *What is wrong with you?* enter your mind, you can respond with: *Anything I have done or will do is covered by Christ's grace.* When the words *You are dirty and worthless* arise, you can speak back with: *Jesus has washed me clean, and in Christ, I have been given supreme worth.* Any condemning thought is met with the comforting words of the gospel. However, in order for us to know these truths, we must be in God's Word daily. We must read and rest in what God's Word says to our shame and know who Scripture declares us to be in Christ. When we remove ourselves from Scripture, we do not have what we need to defend ourselves in the mental battle of shame. God's Word is the shield that prevents shame's arrows from piercing deep into our hearts.

Prayer is also an important part of fighting against thoughts of shame. When condemning thoughts seek to tear us down, we can combat these thoughts with prayer. We can ask God to help us remember and rest in His grace and for His voice to be louder than the condemning voices we hear. Though shameful thoughts wage war in our minds, we are armed in the fight because of the gospel and our mighty God who is with us.

> "GOD'S WORD IS THE SHIELD THAT PREVENTS SHAME'S ARROWS FROM PIERCING DEEP INTO OUR HEARTS."

WEEK FOUR
DAY TWO
QUESTIONS

◆ How does the truth that there is no condemnation in Christ impact you?

◆ What are some thoughts of shame that enter your mind? How does the gospel speak to these thoughts with the truth?

◆ What are some practical ways you can rest in the truth of the gospel when you experience thoughts of shame?

NOTES

IDENTIFYING AND REPLACING THOUGHTS OF SHAME

Philippians 4:8 tells us, "Finally brothers and sisters, whatever is true, whatever is honorable, whatever is just, whatever is pure, whatever is lovely, whatever is commendable—if there is any moral excellence and if there is anything praiseworthy—dwell on these things." This verse encourages us to dwell on what honors the Lord and listen to thoughts that are true and holy. However, the voice of shame can drown the truths we are to dwell on. Often, we can push down this voice or allow it to continue to roar, but identifying thoughts of shame is important. While identifying shameful thoughts can be hard or painful, we need to name our shame in order to deal effectively with our shame. Use this exercise to learn how to identify and replace thoughts of shame with gospel truths.

Identifying Shameful Thoughts
Negative Self-Talk

Shameful thoughts can involve negative self-talk or critical words that we speak about ourselves. We can think these thoughts based on our behavior in certain circumstances or because people have made us feel this way. Some examples of negative self-talk include:

- *I am worthless.*
- *I am not special.*
- *I have nothing of value to contribute.*
- *No one loves me.*
- *I mess up everything.*
- *I am so stupid.*
- *I am a failure.*
- *Something is wrong with me.*

Below, list out any thoughts of negative self-talk you may experience.

Shame-Based Thought Patterns

At times, we may find ourselves stuck in shame-based thought patterns that fixate on what we have done or what others have done to us. Below are some shame-based thought patterns we may experience:

- Dwelling constantly on something you did wrong or you think you did wrong
- Dwelling constantly on words that someone spoke to you
- Replaying in your mind an action you did that was embarrassing
- Replaying a past event in your life that you are ashamed of
- Imagining the judgmental expressions of others that you have received
- Dwelling on other people's past mistakes
- Thinking unkind and shaming words about others

Record any shame-based thought patterns you experience below.

Fear of Man

We all think about how others treat or think about us to some degree, but fear of man can make us enslaved to the thoughts and responses of others. These feelings and fears can stir up shameful thoughts based on our fear of man. Some of these thoughts could be:

- *Those moms think they are better moms than me.*
- *I will never be as good as _____.*
- *If I was more like _____, people would like me more.*
- *They are looking at me because I am weird, unattractive, etc.*
- *I cannot believe I just did that in front of them.*
- *I cannot do this; people will just make fun of me.*

Below, list out any shameful thoughts rooted in fear of man you may experience.

Lies

Identifying shameful thoughts that are lies can be tricky. This is because, sometimes, thoughts that evoke shame come from truthful events or circumstances. Maybe we did mess up in a certain way, or maybe we have a specific weakness that brings us shame. But attached to those true circumstances and weaknesses are shameful thoughts that are not true. A way to distinguish what is a truthful thought and what is a lie is to compare that thought with God's Word. If God's Word speaks against something that we believe about ourselves, it is a lie. For example, one of the previous examples of "I am worthless" is a lie. Because we have been created by God and made in His image, we have worth.

Below, list out any shameful lies you may experience. (Note: You may find that what you have already listed in the above reflections falls under the category of lies. You can repeat those thoughts below if need be).

Replacing Shameful Thoughts

Now that you have done the hard but necessary work of identifying thoughts of shame, it is time to replace those thoughts with gospel truths. What are gospel truths? Gospel truths are what is true because of what Christ has done for us through His death and resurrection. God's Word boasts of these gospel truths, and that is why it is important for us to regularly be in God's Word. Here are some examples of gospel truths:

- *I am chosen by God (John 15:16).*
- *Because of Christ, I am forgiven no matter what I do or have done (Ephesians 1:7).*
- *Christ's grace is sufficient for this weakness (2 Corinthians 12:9).*
- *I am loved by God no matter what is said about me (Romans 8:37–39).*
- *Because of my sin, I will make mistakes, but I am being sanctified by the Holy Spirit (2 Thessalonians 2:13).*

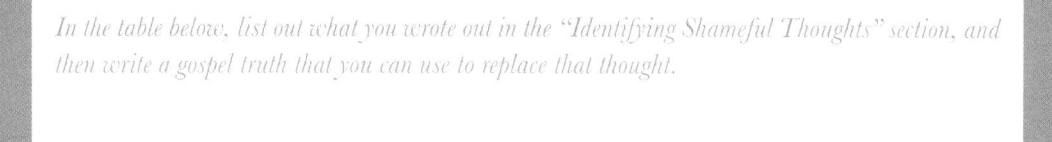

In the table below, list out what you wrote out in the "Identifying Shameful Thoughts" section, and then write a gospel truth that you can use to replace that thought.

If you have trouble thinking of gospel truths, spend some time in prayer, asking God to help you recall truths from His Word. Open up God's Word and see what Scripture says to your thoughts of shame, or look up the Scriptures you have read in this study. (To get started, consider looking up Romans 8:1, Isaiah 50:7, and 1 John 1:9.) You can even ask a fellow believer what gospel truths they know that combat these thoughts. And remember that making a list and changing our thought patterns cannot fully eliminate change—that sort of transformation can only come from the work of the Holy Spirit in us. So, trust in Him as you go about this important task.

Shameful Thought	Gospel Truth

Because we live in a broken world, this process of identifying and replacing shameful thoughts will be a continual process. But the more you dwell in God's Word and meditate on the truths of Scripture, the more prepared you will be to replace shameful thoughts with gospel truths. To meditate on the truths of Scripture simply means to focus deeply on what God's Word says. You can meditate on Scripture by saying certain verses over and over, working through what a verse means, or using Scripture to worship God. Remember, you are not alone in this process because of the Holy Spirit. Rely on His power within you to know, listen, and dwell on what is true.

WEEK FOUR

We keep from *dwelling* on feelings of shame by resting in the *work of Christ.*

DAY THREE

Week Four
Day Three

Read Ephesians 1:3–10.

Practice this week's memory verse.

RESTING IN THE WORK OF CHRIST

Throughout this study, we have seen how much the gospel impacts our shame. The gospel meets us in so many areas of our lives and declares incredible truth over the shame we may feel. In our efforts to combat our shame with the gospel, we must reflect on what Christ has done for us. We keep from dwelling on feelings of shame by resting in the work of Christ. But before we dive into the implications of the work of Christ for our shame, we must first understand what the work of Christ is and includes.

When we talk about the work of Christ, we refer to what Jesus did during His ministry and accomplished through His death and resurrection. Most of the time, the phrase "the work of Christ" is used when discussing Christ's sacrifice on the cross and the forgiveness and salvation He made possible through His death. When we seek to rest in the work of Christ, we do so by asking ourselves, *What has Jesus done for me, and who does He declare me to be in light of what He has done?* While numerous passages of Scripture speak to these truths, Ephesians 1:3–10 beautifully captures the work of Christ and who we are in Christ. Throughout these verses, we receive these treasured truths: in Christ, we are blessed, chosen, adopted, and redeemed.

Paul starts off by declaring that if we are in Christ, God has blessed us with every spiritual blessing (Ephesians 1:3). To be blessed spiritually is far better than to be blessed materially. While some aspects of being blessed spiritually involve what is material, like our eternal inheritance and being co-heirs with Christ (Romans 8:17), Paul is mainly drawing us to all that Christ gives us spiritually. These blessings include peace with God, forgiveness, imperishable hope, and strength. These truths can comfort us if we feel shame for not having enough. Maybe we feel shame about our past mistakes or the way others have treated us. Whatever our story with shame, the fact that we have every spiritual blessing in Christ reminds us that, in Christ, we have everything that we need. Those who seem to be thriving physically—meaning they have health and wealth—but do not have a relationship with the Lord are not truly thriving. Therefore, we can rest in the truth that we are blessed in Christ even if there are areas of lack in our lives.

Paul also reminds us that we are chosen (Ephesians 1:4). To be chosen by God is to be gifted with salvation. According to His unconditional love and perfect sovereignty, God chose those of us in Christ to receive salvation. Being chosen by God is far greater than being chosen by mankind. While many people might boast in their relationships or positions, the relationship we have with God and our position with Christ is greater. Why? Because our relationship and position with God is perfect and permanent. Not only this but if we are in Christ, we have been chosen by God, all because of God's grace. We did not earn our salvation, nor did we possess any quality that made us "worth" saving. If we experience any shame for being rejected or overlooked, the truth that we are chosen in Christ gives us peace. Even if we have been cast aside by man—we are chosen by God.

Connected with the truth that we are chosen in Christ is the truth that we have been adopted through Christ (Ephesians 1:5). To be adopted means to have been brought into the family of God. Therefore, those of us who are chosen by God are declared children of God. If we are in Christ, God is our Father, and we will experience the fullness of Him being our Father and part of His family when we dwell with Him forever. This truth comforts those of us who feel shame due to our familial situations. Maybe we have been abandoned or mistreated by a family member, and we feel shame. Even though these situations are painful, we can rest in the incredible truth that we are children of God. As God's children, we are held in the hands of our loving and compassionate Father.

Lastly, Paul proclaims that we have been redeemed in Christ. He writes in verse 7 that in Christ, "we have redemption through his blood, the forgiveness of our trespasses." To be redeemed is to be set free from sin because Christ experienced the punishment for our sin. Christ took our place on the cross, which means that He received the punishment each one of us deserves for our sin. The blood of Christ washes us clean and sets us free from our sin. To be set free from our sin also means that we are no longer declared guilty of our sin. Christ's grace causes us to be blameless in the eyes of God. Therefore, if we feel or receive shame for our sin, we can remind ourselves that we are forgiven in Christ. We are redeemed by Christ, no matter what we have done or what others have accused us of doing.

This passage drips of Christ's grace and God's love, and it should cause us to proclaim with Paul the opening words of this passage: "Blessed is the God and Father of our Lord Jesus Christ." All of these incredible gifts and blessings are given to us because of the work of Christ and the love of our Father. When we are ashamed, let us rest in the truths of who we are in Christ. Let us rest in who Jesus declares us to be when shame accuses and berates us. In every situation of shame, you can confidently say, *In Christ, I am blessed, chosen, adopted, and redeemed.*

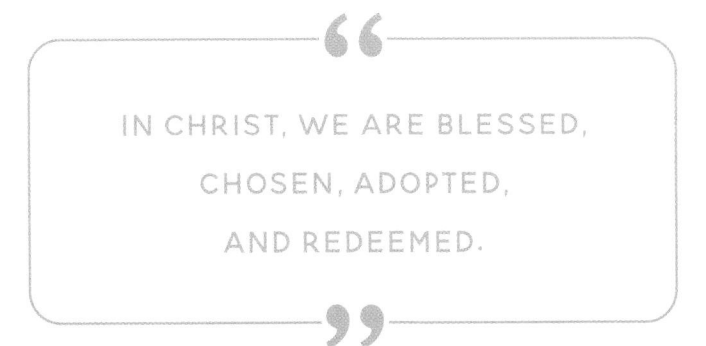

> IN CHRIST, WE ARE BLESSED, CHOSEN, ADOPTED, AND REDEEMED.

WEEK FOUR DAY THREE QUESTIONS

◆ How do these truths from Ephesians 1:3–10 impact any current feelings of shame?

◆ In what ways does Ephesians 1:3–10 make you grateful for Jesus and what He has done for you?

◆ What does it look like practically for you to rest in the work of Christ?

NOTES

WEEK FOUR

God's grace is *sufficient* **for every experience of** *shame.*

DAY FOUR

Week Four
Day Four

Read Galatians 2:15–21.

Practice this week's memory verse.

RECEIVING THE GRACE OF GOD

One of the greatest gifts given to us through Christ is grace. We did not earn God's grace, nor did we deserve God's grace, but it is given to every person who trusts and believes in Jesus. However, it is possible for some people to think that they can receive God's favor in other ways. Throughout his letters, Paul regularly warned of teachers who proclaimed that salvation came from works of the Law instead of by faith through grace alone. And in some ways, we can think this way today. Understanding Christ's grace as a free gift might seem too incredible to us, so we might be tempted to believe that we must merit it by our own efforts. Some of us might also think that we are too sinful to receive God's grace. Our shame might make us feel disqualified from Christ's grace and forgiveness. But the grace of God is freely given to anyone who trusts in Jesus and is based on the work of Christ alone.

Paul writes in Galatians 2:15–21 how no one is justified by the works of the Law but by faith in Jesus. Through these words, Paul refutes the belief that strict adherence to the Law secures salvation or that works of the Law declare people innocent of their sin. A more modern way to express this belief would be to view one's good works or obedience to God as what saves. But our works do not save us. It is faith in Jesus and His sacrifice for us that bring us salvation. This is an incredibly freeing truth. If God's grace was attainable by our own merit, we would be burdened by the weight of doing everything right so that we could have God's favor. But the grace of Christ gives us freedom. We are free from the thinking that our works save us and are free to obey the Lord without the pressure to be perfect.

Even if we accept the free gift of God's grace, we should be careful not to rely on our works as a means to maintain God's grace. If we received God's grace based on the work of Christ alone, then we are kept by God's grace because of Christ's work. Yet it is possible for us to struggle with receiving God's grace on a daily basis. We might believe that Christ has saved us yet still wrestle with the truth that we continuously receive God's grace. Perhaps we feel this way because certain instances of shame make us believe that we no longer have God's grace. In response, we seek to do all we can in our own power to maintain the grace of God. But this, too, is exhausting, and operating in this way keeps us from walking in the freedom we have received from Christ.

Because Christ's grace is permanently poured out upon us, we can rest in Christ's grace instead of trying to keep God's grace by our power. When shame arises, we can remember that God's grace is ours always, no matter what we have done, what has been to us, or any offense that is brought up against us. If shame keeps us from believing Christ's grace is ours, we need to walk in the grace we have received from Christ.

One way that we walk in the grace of God is by living for God. Paul writes in verse 20 how he has been crucified with Christ, and it is no longer Paul who lives but Christ who lives in him. This incredible union transforms Paul's allegiance and causes him to declare how he lives by faith in Jesus. This means that Paul desires to give his life completely to Christ, responding to the grace he received by serving the Lord rather than serving and living for himself. Like Paul, each one of us in Christ has been "crucified." Our old, sinful selves have died, and we now live as new creations with the Spirit of God inside of us. As new creations, we respond to the life-transforming grace of Jesus by serving and worshiping Him. And we do so by faith, continuously trusting in the One who gave His life for us.

The fact that our old selves have been crucified with Christ comforts us when we feel ashamed of our past. If our old selves are gone, we are no longer guilty of the sins we have committed. The sins of the past do not nullify the grace of God. The enemy may bring up these sins against us, but Christ's grace has washed these sins away. In Christ, we are new, so let us focus on the new creation we are in Christ more than on who we used to be without Him.

Another aspect of walking in God's grace is refusing to set aside the grace of God. Paul writes in verse 21 how he will not set aside God's grace or see it as invalid or insufficient. It is possible for us to set aside God's grace in our moments of shame. We do so by not believing that God's grace is powerful enough to cover the shame brought about by insecurities, failures, and accusations. But God's grace is sufficient for every experience of shame (2 Corinthians 12:9). We have God's grace even on our worst days and in our worst failures. Therefore, we can see God's grace as "enough" for anything that stirs up shame in our lives.

In our struggles with shame, we must regularly recall and rest in the grace of God. In doing so, we will be grateful for how Christ has given us His grace and sustains us by His grace, no matter our sins and struggles. We will be freed to serve the Lord and live for Him without shame holding us back. If we are in Christ, we have received the grace of God, and His grace changes everything about how we live.

> IF WE ARE IN CHRIST, WE HAVE RECEIVED THE GRACE OF GOD, AND HIS GRACE CHANGES EVERYTHING.

WEEK FOUR
DAY FOUR
QUESTIONS

◆ Why is it important to believe that God's grace is given through Christ alone?

◆ How does knowing how grace is received impact how you view Christ's grace daily?

◆ How should you live in light of the truth that your old self has been crucified?

NOTES

WEEK FOUR

♦

Our hope **for the struggle against shame lies in the** *eternity* **to come.**

DAY FIVE

Week Four
Day Five

Read Revelation 21:1–7 and 1 Peter 1:3–5.

Practice this week's memory verse.

HOPE FOR SHAME

As followers of Christ, we live in what is called "the already but not yet." This means that God's kingdom is here but is not yet fully realized. Because God's kingdom has not been fully realized, we still live in a world tainted by sin. While Christ has defeated sin and death on the cross, sin and death are still a reality until Jesus comes back to remove both once and for all. As believers, we live in this tension of experiencing the life and blessings God gives us while struggling against a sinful flesh. Until Christ returns, shame will continue to scream. Shame will continue to tap us on the shoulder, letting us know that it is still here. Yet our hope for the struggle against shame lies in the eternity to come. Christ will return to set all things right, and when He does, shame will be erased forever.

Revelation 21:1–7 gives us a glimpse of what will be a reality for every follower of Christ. Heaven will come to meet earth fully and perfectly, and God will dwell with His people. He will wipe all our tears away, and there will be no more death, grief, pain, and sin—forever. All the dark and detestable things of this earth will pass away, for God will make all things new. This future reality brings us so much hope, and one way this picture gives us hope is through the promise of removal.

The picture of God wiping away our tears is a picture of what He will do for everything that is broken and sinful. He will clear all brokenness and unrighteousness permanently. This means that all of our feelings and thoughts of shame, as well as anything that currently shames us, will be gone. With sin and shame permanently removed, we will live in perfect peace. We will nestle deeply within the arms of grace forever, no more experiencing the sting of shame. Revelation 21:1–7 teaches us that this removal is God's work. He is the One who will make all things new and clear the shame that currently lingers.

This future removal gives us hope that shame will not always remain. Though shame may taunt and accuse now, one day, the voice of shame will be silenced forever. This truth encourages us to look confidently in the face of shame. Christ's sacrifice on the cross has proven that sin and shame hold no power over us, and our eternity to come declares final victory over our sin and shame. We can live confidently in the present, even with the presence of shame, knowing that Jesus will make all things new.

Jesus will not only make the whole world new, but He will also make us new. He will transform us, and we will be glorified, which means that we will be cleansed from all of our sin. We will be the holy people God created us to be, and we will have no spot or stain of sin again. Revelation 3:5 tells us that those who belong to Jesus will be clothed in white. This imagery describes the purity believers will have because sin has been removed from them. The promise of being covered with garments of righteousness points us back to the garden of Eden. When Adam and Eve sinned and were ashamed of their nakedness, God clothed them (Genesis 3:21). Though we have already been clothed by Christ's righteousness through His sacrifice, the fullness of this covering will be experienced in the future. We will be completely cleansed and deemed perfectly pure in the eyes of God.

We anticipate the day when we will be made fully righteous, but we can cling to the truth that we possess the righteousness of Christ. In the moments when shame rears its head, we can be comforted by the truth that we have been clothed by Christ and will be further clothed one day. We are forgiven and declared innocent, no matter what shame tells us. We can look back at the cross with gratitude and toward eternity with joy because of the promised cleansing of Christ.

The cleansing of Christ also encourages us that we have closeness with the Lord. Shame separates, but Christ's grace unites. Because of Jesus, we have an intimate relationship with the Lord that cannot be taken away. And when Christ returns, we will dwell with the full presence of God forever. He will be our God, and we will be His people (Revelation 21:3). Without Jesus, the thought of God's presence would make us shrink away in shame. Like Adam and Eve, we seek to hide because of our shame, but with our shame removed by Christ, we will never feel like we need to hide from God. We will embrace His closeness with joy, knowing that there is nothing that separates us. We can allow this picture of intimacy and unity to remind us how we have God's presence with us here and now. Even though we struggle with sin and shame, God remains near to us because of the grace of Jesus. There is no need for us to hide from the Lord, for we are invited into His presence as sons and daughters of God.

Though shame hurts us in the present, we can have hope as we rest in the future removal of shame and the promised cleansing and closeness we will receive. Until Christ returns, we can be strengthened and comforted as we trust in what Jesus has done for us and look forward to what He will do for us. So we remain steadfast as we wait, fixed solely on the promise that God will make all things new and that shame will not have the final word.

> THOUGH SHAME MAY TAUNT AND ACCUSE NOW, ONE DAY, THE VOICE OF SHAME WILL BE SILENCED FOREVER.

WEEK FOUR DAY FIVE QUESTIONS

◆ Read Joel 2:26–27. How is this promise ultimately fulfilled through Christ's second coming?

◆ In what ways do the promises of eternity give you hope as you battle against shame? Spend some time in prayer, thanking God for the hope He has given you.

NOTES

END-OF-WEEK REFLECTION

Think back on all of the Scripture that you read and studied this week as you answer the questions below.

What did you observe about God and His character?

What did you learn about the condition of mankind and yourself?

How does this week's Scripture point to the gospel?

Week Four
Day Five

How do the truths you have learned this week about God, man, and the gospel give you hope, peace, or encouragement?

How should you respond to what you read and learned this week? Write down one or two specific action steps you can take this week to apply what you learned. Then, write a prayer in response to your study of God's Word.

WEEK FOUR APPLICATION QUESTIONS

Take some time to apply and share the truths of Scripture you learned this week. Here are a few ideas of how you could do this:

- Schedule a meet-up with a friend to share what you are learning from God's Word.

- Use these prompts to journal or pray through what God is revealing to you through your study of His Word.

Lord, I feel…

Lord, You are…

Lord, forgive me for…

Lord, help me with…

Week Four
Days Six + Seven

- Spend time worshiping God in a way that is meaningful to you, whether that is taking a walk in nature, painting, drawing, singing, etc.

- Paraphrase the Scripture you read this week.

- Use a study Bible or commentary to help you answer questions that came up as you read this week's Scripture.

- Take steps to fulfill the action steps you listed on Day 5.

- Use highlighters to mark the places you see the metanarrative of Scripture in one or more of the passages of Scripture that you read this week. (See *The Metanarrative of Scripture* on page 14.)

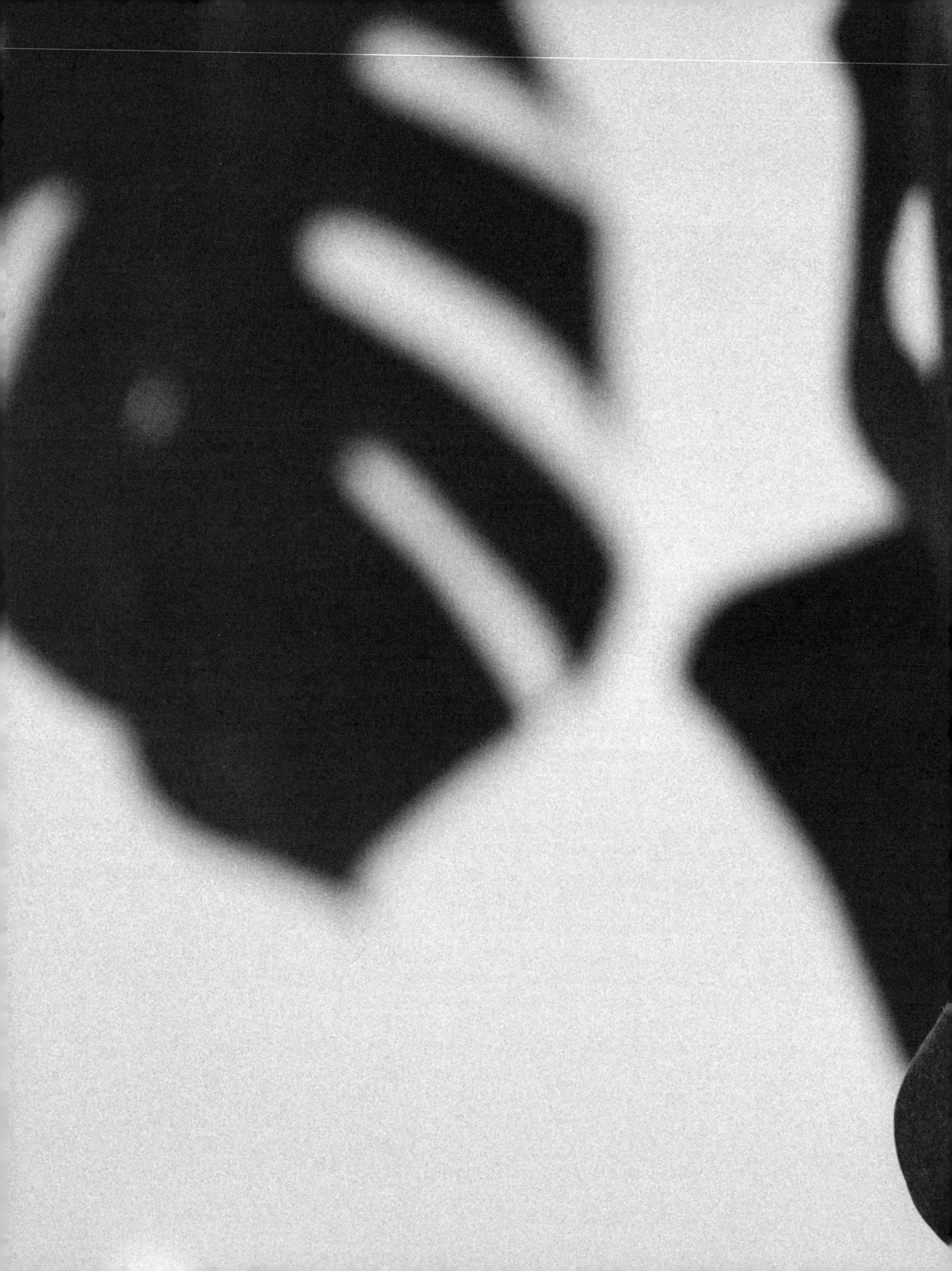

FREE FROM SHAME

IN OUR STRUGGLES WITH SHAME, WE MUST REGULARLY RECALL AND REST IN THE GRACE OF GOD.

WHAT IS THE GOSPEL?

Thank you for reading and enjoying this study with us! We are abundantly grateful for the Word of God, the instruction we glean from it, and the ever-growing understanding it provides for us of God's character. We are also thankful that Scripture continually points to one thing in innumerable ways: the gospel.

We remember our brokenness when we read about the fall of Adam and Eve in the garden of Eden (Genesis 3), where sin entered into a perfect world and maimed it. We remember the necessity that something innocent must die to pay for our sin when we read about the atoning sacrifices in the Old Testament. We read that we have all sinned and fallen short of the glory of God (Romans 3:23) and that the penalty for our brokenness, the wages of our sin, is death (Romans 6:23). We all need grace and mercy, but most importantly, we all need a Savior.

We consider the goodness of God when we realize that He did not plan to leave us in this dire state. We see His promise to buy us back from the clutches of sin and death in Genesis 3:15. And we see that promise accomplished with Jesus Christ on the cross. Jesus Christ knew no sin yet became sin so that we might become righteous through His sacrifice (2 Corinthians 5:21). Jesus was tempted in every way that we are and lived sinlessly. He was reviled yet still yielded Himself for our sake, that we may have life abundant in Him. Jesus lived the perfect life that we could not live and died the death that we deserved.

The gospel is profound yet simple. There are many mysteries in it that we will never understand this side of heaven, but there is still overwhelming weight to its implications in this life. The gospel tells of our sinfulness and God's goodness and a gracious gift that compels a response. We are saved by grace through faith, which means that we rest with faith in the grace that Jesus Christ displayed on the cross (Ephesians 2:8–9). We cannot save ourselves from our brokenness or do any amount of good works to merit God's favor. Still, we can have faith that what Jesus accomplished in His death, burial, and resurrection was more than enough for our salvation and our eternal delight. When we accept God, we are commanded to die to ourselves and our sinful desires and live a life worthy of the calling we have received (Ephesians 4:1). The gospel compels us to be sanctified, and in so doing, we are conformed to the likeness of Christ Himself. This is hope. This is redemption. This is the gospel.

SCRIPTURES TO REFERENCE

GENESIS 3:15

I will put hostility between you and the woman, and between your offspring and her offspring. He will strike your head, and you will strike his heel.

ROMANS 3:23

For all have sinned and fall short of the glory of God.

ROMANS 6:23

For the wages of sin is death, but the gift of God is eternal life in Christ Jesus our Lord.

2 CORINTHIANS 5:21

He made the one who did not know sin to be sin for us, so that in him we might become the righteousness of God.

EPHESIANS 2:8-9

For you are saved by grace through faith, and this is not from yourselves; it is God's gift — not from works, so that no one can boast.

EPHESIANS 4:1-3

Therefore I, the prisoner in the Lord, urge you to walk worthy of the calling you have received, with all humility and gentleness, with patience, bearing with one another in love, making every effort to keep the unity of the Spirit through the bond of peace.

BIBLIOGRAPHY

Week 1

Ligonier Ministries. "The Fall of Adam." *Ligonier.* Updated January 14, 2010. https://www.ligonier.org/learn/devotionals/fall-adam.

Ligonier Ministries. "The Righteousness of David." *Ligonier.* Updated July 13, 2019. https://www.ligonier.org/learn/devotionals/righteousness-of-david.

Sproul, R.C. "Jesus Became a Curse for Us." *Ligonier.* Ligonier Ministries. April 2, 2021. https://www.ligonier.org/posts/supreme-malediction-jesus-became-curse.

Sproul, R.C., ed. *The Reformation Study Bible.* Sanford, FL: Reformation Trust Publishing, 2015.

Week 2

Akin, Daniel L. *Christ-Centered Exposition Commentary: Exalting Jesus in Mark.* Edited by David Platt, Daniel L. Akin, and Tony Merida, 112-113. Nashville: B&H Publishing Group, 2014.

Carter, Matt, and Josh Wredberg. *Christ-Centered Exposition Commentary: Exalting Jesus in John.* Edited by David Platt, Daniel L. Akin, and Tony Merida, 183-185. Nashville: B&H Publishing Group, 2017.

Hamilton, Victor P. *The New International Commentary of the Old Testament: The Book of Genesis 1–17.* Grand Rapids: Eerdmans, 1990.

Piper, John. "The Image of God: An Approach from Biblical and Systematic Theology." Desiring God. Originally published in Studia Biblica et Theologica. March 1971. https://www.desiringgod.org/articles/the-image-of-god.

Sailhamer, John H. *The Expositor's Bible Commentary Volume 2: Genesis.* Edited by Frank E. Gaebelein, 132-135. Grand Rapids: Zondervan, 1990.

Tenney, Merrill C. *The Expositor's Bible Commentary Volume 9: John and Acts.* Edited by Frank E. Gaebelein, 89-91. Grand Rapids: Zondervan, 1981.

Thomas, Heath, and J. D. Greear. *Christ-Centered Exposition Commentary: Exalting Jesus in 1 & 2 Samuel.* Edited by David Platt, Daniel L. Akin, and Tony Merida, 36-58. Nashville: B&H Publishing Group, 2016.

Wessel, Walter W. *The Expositor's Bible Commentary Volume 8: Matthew, Mark, Luke.* Edited by Frank E. Gaebelein, 660-661. Grand Rapids: Zondervan, 1984.

Wood, Leon J. *The Expositor's Bible Commentary Volume 7: Daniel through the Minor Prophets.* Edited by Frank E. Gaebelein, 170-225. Grand Rapids: Zondervan, 1985.

Youngblood, Ronald F. *The Expositor's Bible Commentary Volume 3: 1 & 2 Samuel.* Edited by Frank E. Gaebelein, 569-582. Grand Rapids: Zondervan, 1992.

Week 3

Beck, John A., David G. Hansen, and James C. Martin. *A Visual Guide to Gospel Events.* Grand Rapids: Baker Books, 2010.

Kostenberger, Andreas J. "John." In *Christian Standard Study Bible*, edited by Edwin A. Blum and Trevin Wax, 1661-1711. Nashville: Holman Bible Publishers, 2017.

Piper, John. "What Does It Mean for Jesus to Despise Shame?" March 29, 2013. Desiring God. https://www.desiringgod.org/articles/what-does-it-mean-for-jesus-to-despise-shame.

Week 4

Chappell, Christine. "Hope + Help for Shame & Regret with Ed Welch." February 28, 2022. In *Hope + Help*. Produced by The Institute for Biblical Counseling & Discipleship. MP3 Audio, 51:52. https://open.spotify.com/episode/2nwKCrOpFIrb1MbHb8dSuU?si=Pi-YV94NEQP2l2eN-13zmPg.

Cole, Alan R. *Tyndale New Testament Commentary: Galatians: An Introduction and Commentary Volume 9.* Downers Grove, IL: InterVarsity Press, 1989.

Foulkes, Francis. *Tyndale New Testament Commentary: Ephesians: An Introduction and Commentary Volume 10.* Downers Grove, IL: InterVarsity Press, 1989.

Morris, Leon. *The Pillar New Testament Commentary: The Epistle to the Romans.* Grand Rapids, MI; Leicester, England: W.B. Eerdmans; InterVarsity Press, 1988.

Moyter, Alec J. *Tyndale Old Testament Commentary: Isaiah: An Introduction and Commentary Volume 20.* Downers Grove, IL: InterVarsity Press, 1999.

Thank you for studying
God's Word with us

CONNECT WITH US
@thedailygraceco
@dailygracepodcast

CONTACT US
info@thedailygraceco.com

SHARE
#thedailygraceco

VISIT US ONLINE
www.thedailygraceco.com

MORE DAILY GRACE
Daily Grace® Podcast